I0436534

Chapter 6: After the Submission

- The Review Process Explained

- Handling Rejections and Feedback

- Resubmission Strategies

Chapter 7: Managing Grant Funds

- Effective Fund Management Strategies

- Reporting and Compliance

- Maximizing the Impact of the Grant

Chapter 8: Success Stories and Case Studies

- Interviews with Successful Grantees

- Analysis of Successful Proposals

- Lessons Learned

Chapter 9: Advanced Strategies

- Building Long-term Relationships with Funders

- Leveraging Grants for Further Funding

- The Role of Partnerships and Collaborations

Chapter 10: The Future of Grant Funding

- Emerging Trends in Grant Funding

- The Impact of Technology on Grant Seeking

- Predictions for the Business Grant Landscape

Appendices

- Glossary of Grant Terms

- List of Resources and Tools

- Templates and Sample Documents

Conclusion

Preface

Introduction to Grant Funding

Welcome to the world of grant funding, an arena where ambition meets opportunity, and ideas find their financial wings. This book is designed to be your comprehensive guide through the intricate and often daunting landscape of securing grants for your business. Grant funding, a vital tool for business growth and innovation, is often underutilized due to a lack of understanding and accessibility. Our goal is to demystify this process and provide you with the knowledge and tools needed to unlock the potential of grant funding.

What is Grant Funding?

At its core, grant funding is the provision of financial assistance from organizations - typically governments, corporations, or foundations - to businesses, non-profits, or individuals. Unlike loans, grants do not require repayment, making them an exceptionally attractive source of funding for businesses looking to expand, innovate, or launch new projects without the burden of additional debt.

Why Grant Funding?

For businesses, grant funding can be a game-changer. It can provide the necessary capital to jumpstart growth, fund research and development, or expand into new markets. Grants can also offer a sense of credibility and

Grant Funding Unlocked: A Business Guide to Securing Funds"

Contents

Expanded Table of Contents

validation, opening doors to further investment and partnership opportunities.

Navigating the Grant Funding Landscape

The path to securing grant funding is often complex and competitive. It involves understanding different types of grants, identifying the right opportunities, crafting compelling applications, and managing funds effectively upon award. This journey requires not only a solid understanding of the grant funding process but also a strategic approach tailored to your business's unique needs and goals.

Purpose of This Book

This book aims to serve as your navigator in the journey of grant funding. Whether you are a startup founder, a small business owner, or part of a large corporation, the insights and strategies provided here will equip you to effectively seek and manage grant funding. From the basics of understanding what grants are to the nuances of application and compliance, we cover it all.

We begin by exploring the foundational aspects of grant funding - what it is, its importance, and the different types available. As we progress, we delve into the practical steps of preparing for and applying to grants, managing the funds received, and leveraging these opportunities for long-term business growth.

Embark on the Journey

As you turn these pages, you will find not only information but also inspiration from real-life success stories and practical advice. Grant funding is more than just financial aid; it's a catalyst for innovation and growth. Let this book be your guide to unlocking the potential of grant funding for your business.

Welcome to the journey. Let's embark on this path to unlocking new opportunities and achieving business success through the power of grant funding.

Importance for Businesses

In the ever-evolving landscape of business, securing a competitive edge often hinges on access to capital. Grant funding emerges as a crucial element in this context, offering a lifeline of financial support that can propel businesses towards their goals. This section explores the multifaceted importance of grant funding for businesses of all sizes and stages.

1. Financial Leverage Without Debt

One of the most significant advantages of grant funding is that it provides financial resources without the obligation of repayment. Unlike loans, grants do not accrue interest nor do they require collateral. This aspect of grant funding makes it an ideal source of capital for businesses looking to expand or innovate without increasing their debt burden.

2. Opportunity for Innovation and Growth

Grants often target specific areas such as research and development, technological advancements, or entering new markets. Access to this funding allows businesses to undertake projects that might have been too risky or expensive to consider otherwise. This can lead to innovation, differentiation in the market, and ultimately, business growth.

3. Validation and Credibility

Receiving a grant, especially from a reputable organization, serves as a stamp of approval for a business's vision and potential. This validation can be a powerful tool in attracting additional investment, forming partnerships, and building a strong reputation in the industry.

4. Access to Networks and Expertise

Many grant programs offer more than just financial assistance. They provide opportunities to connect with mentors, industry experts, and a network of peers. Such connections can be invaluable for gaining insights, exploring collaborative opportunities, and enhancing the business's profile.

5. Encouraging Social Responsibility and Sustainability

Grants often encourage businesses to focus on social responsibility and sustainable practices. By aligning business goals with these principles, companies not only contribute positively to society and the environment but also align with the growing global emphasis on responsible business practices.

6. Mitigating Risk

For businesses, especially startups and SMEs, the risk is a constant companion. Grant funding can help mitigate some of this risk by providing the necessary funds to explore new ideas, enter new markets, or invest in essential technology without risking the company's financial stability.

7. Enabling Long-Term Planning

With the financial backing of grants, businesses can plan for the long term. This stability allows for more strategic decision-making, focused investments in key areas, and the development of a sustainable business model.

In summary, grant funding is not just about financial aid; it's a catalyst that can drive business success in multiple ways. It offers a blend of financial support, opportunities for innovation, increased credibility, access to networks, a platform for responsible growth, risk mitigation, and a foundation for long-term strategic planning. Understanding and leveraging grant funding can, therefore, be a decisive factor in a business's journey towards success and sustainability.

Overview of the Book

This book is structured to provide a comprehensive guide on navigating the intricate world of grant funding for businesses. It is designed to be both informative and practical, offering insights, strategies, and tools to effectively secure and manage grant funding. Each chapter focuses on a specific aspect of the grant funding process, ensuring a thorough understanding from the foundational concepts to the advanced strategies. Here is an overview of what you can expect in each chapter:

Chapter 1: Understanding Grant Funding

This chapter lays the groundwork by explaining what grant funding is, the different types of grants available, and their role in supporting business growth. It provides a clear foundation for the rest of the book.

Chapter 2: Preparing for Grants

Learn how to assess your business's needs and align them with the right grant opportunities. This chapter covers the initial steps of preparing for grant applications, including understanding eligibility criteria.

Chapter 3: Researching Grants

Discover how to effectively find and select relevant grants. This chapter guides you through using online databases, resources, and networking to identify the best opportunities for your business.

Chapter 4: Crafting a Winning Proposal

A deep dive into the art and science of writing a compelling grant proposal. It includes tips on creating a persuasive narrative, budgeting, and presenting your business case effectively.

Chapter 5: The Application Process

This chapter outlines the application process, highlighting common mistakes to avoid and offering strategies for submitting a strong application that stands out.

Chapter 6: After the Submission

Learn what happens after you submit your application, including the review process, how to handle rejections, and strategies for resubmission.

Chapter 7: Managing Grant Funds

Once successful, managing grant funds effectively is crucial. This chapter provides strategies for fund management, compliance, and reporting, ensuring you maximize the impact of the grant.

Chapter 8: Success Stories and Case Studies
Real-life examples and interviews with successful grantees offer inspiration and practical insights. This chapter analyzes successful proposals and highlights key lessons learned.

Chapter 9: Advanced Strategies
For those looking to go a step further, this chapter covers advanced strategies like building long-term relationships with funders and leveraging grants for further funding.

Chapter 10: The Future of Grant Funding
Explore emerging trends in grant funding, the impact of technology, and predictions for the future of business grants.

Appendices
A valuable resource section including a glossary, list of tools and resources, and sample templates and documents to aid in your grant application process.

Conclusion
A recap of the key points and final thoughts to inspire and motivate readers in their pursuit of grant funding.

About the Author

Bernard Baah, the dynamic CEO of Filly Coder, is a distinguished professional with a rich academic background and extensive experience in grant proposal writing. He earned his Bachelor of Science in Civil Engineering from the University of Vermont, a Master of Science in Construction Management from Stanford University, and an MBA from Ohio State University.

At the helm of Filly Coder, a leading software development company (https://fillycoder.com), Bernard has demonstrated exceptional skill in grant proposal writing. His expertise extends beyond securing funding for his startups, assisting numerous clients in acquiring grants for their projects.

Bernard's combination of engineering insight, construction management skills, and business acumen positions him as an authority in grant funding. His impact in this field goes beyond practical applications; he is a regular contributor to workshops, seminars, and industry publications.

His book, "Grant Funding Unlocked: A Business Guide to Securing Funds," is a testament to his deep understanding of the grant-seeking process, designed to empower businesses of all sizes with essential strategies for navigating grant funding complexities.

Beyond his professional realm, Bernard is dedicated to mentoring emerging entrepreneurs and is deeply involved in community development. He is committed to driving Filly Coder's mission forward. In his free time, he enjoys traveling, reading, and creating cherished memories with family and friends.

Chapter 1: Understanding Grant Funding

Definition of Grant Funding

At the heart of any discussion about grant funding is the need to understand precisely what it entails. Grant funding is more than just financial assistance; it's a multifaceted tool for fostering innovation, growth, and social impact in the business world.

What is Grant Funding?

Grant funding can be defined as the allocation of financial resources by an organization – typically governments, corporations, foundations, or trusts – to a recipient, usually businesses, non-profit organizations, or individuals, to support specific projects or initiatives. Unlike loans, grants are not required to be repaid, making them an attractive form of financing for many businesses.

Key Characteristics of Grant Funding

- **Non-repayable**: Grants do not need to be paid back, distinguishing them from loans or other types of financing that burden the recipient with debt.

- **Targeted Purposes**: Grants are often designated for specific purposes or projects. They might support research and development, technological advancements, social initiatives, or expansion into new markets.

- **Competitive and Conditional**: Securing a grant is typically competitive, with applicants required to meet specific criteria and undergo a rigorous selection process. Moreover, grants usually come with conditions regarding how the funds are to be used.

- **Varied Sources**: Grants are available from a diverse range of sources. Government agencies, international organizations, private corporations, and philanthropic foundations are common grant providers.

Importance in the Business Context

In a business context, grant funding serves as a critical catalyst for growth and innovation. It provides financial breathing room for companies to explore new ideas, invest in research and development, or expand operations without the immediate pressure of profitability or return on investment that other forms of financing might demand.

A Tool for Strategic Development

Beyond mere financial aid, grant funding can be seen as a strategic development tool. It allows businesses to undertake projects that align with broader economic, social, or environmental goals, fostering a more holistic approach to business growth. This alignment can also enhance a company's reputation and market position, as it demonstrates a commitment to more than just profit.

Understanding grant funding in its entirety is the first step in harnessing its potential. It's not just about the funds; it's about understanding the opportunity and responsibility that comes with them. This chapter sets the foundation for exploring how businesses can effectively identify, apply for, and manage grant funding to achieve their goals and contribute to broader societal objectives.

Types of Grants (Government, Corporate, Non-profit)

In the realm of grant funding, it's essential to recognize the diversity in the types of grants available. Each type comes from different sources, each with its own set of objectives, requirements, and application processes. Broadly, grants can be categorized into three main types: Government, Corporate, and Non-profit.

1. Government Grants

- **Definition**: Government grants are funds provided by local, state, or federal government bodies. They are typically aimed at promoting specific public benefits, such as economic development, scientific research, or social welfare.

- **Characteristics**:

- Often have stringent eligibility and compliance requirements.

- Usually focused on larger societal goals like job creation, innovation, community development, or environmental conservation.

- Tend to have detailed application processes.

- **Examples**: Small Business Innovation Research (SBIR) grants, Community Development Block Grants.

2. Corporate Grants

- **Definition**: Corporate grants are funds allocated by businesses as part of their corporate social responsibility (CSR) initiatives or philanthropic efforts. These grants are often directed towards projects that align with the company's values or business interests.

- **Characteristics**:

  - Often seek to support initiatives related to education, health, environmental sustainability, or community development.

  - May offer additional resources like mentorship, networking opportunities, or in-kind support.

  - Can be more flexible in terms of project scope and funding usage.

- **Examples**: Grants from companies like Google, Microsoft, or Coca-Cola that focus on technology, education, or community welfare.

3. Non-profit Grants

- **Definition**: Non-profit grants are distributed by foundations, trusts, or charitable organizations. These grants are typically funded by endowments or donations and focus on supporting social, educational, health, or environmental causes.

- **Characteristics**:

- Usually emphasize innovation, community impact, or research.

- Often have a particular focus or niche, such as supporting underserved communities, advancing medical research, or promoting arts and culture.

- Application processes can vary significantly depending on the organization's size and focus.

- **Examples**: Grants from the Ford Foundation, Rockefeller Foundation, or local community foundations.

Navigating the Different Types

Understanding the nuances of these different types of grants is crucial for businesses. Each type of grant has its own culture, expectations, and application process. Businesses must align their goals with the grant's objectives, understand the specific requirements, and tailor their applications accordingly.

The landscape of grant funding is diverse and rich with opportunities. By understanding the different types of grants available and their unique characteristics, businesses can strategically identify the ones that best align with their goals and projects. This understanding forms the basis for effectively navigating the grant application process, which we will explore in the subsequent chapters.

The Role of Grants in Business Growth

Grants play a pivotal role in the growth and development of businesses, offering more than just financial assistance. This section delves into the various ways that grants contribute to business growth, underscoring their significance in the broader business landscape.

1. Catalyzing Innovation and Research

- **Driving Research and Development**: Grants, particularly in industries like technology, healthcare, and environmental sciences, can provide the necessary capital for research and development.

This funding enables businesses to undertake innovative projects, develop new products, or improve existing services.

- **Encouraging Risk-taking**: With the financial safety net that grants provide, businesses can afford to take risks on innovative projects that might not have been feasible otherwise.

2. Enhancing Business Credibility and Reputation

- **Validation of Business Concepts**: Receiving a grant, especially from a reputable source, can serve as a powerful endorsement of the business's potential and the viability of its ideas.

- **Attracting Further Investment**: This credibility can be instrumental in attracting additional investment from other sources, such as venture capitalists, angel investors, or banks.

3. Facilitating Market Expansion and Growth

- **Support for Scaling Operations**: Grants can enable businesses to expand their operations, enter new markets, or increase production capacity without the financial strain typically associated with such growth.

- **Building Infrastructure**: They can also be used to build necessary infrastructure, such as manufacturing facilities, laboratories, or IT systems, which are essential for business expansion.

4. Promoting Social Responsibility and Environmental Sustainability

- **Encouraging Responsible Practices**: Many grants are aimed at promoting social and environmental responsibility. Businesses can use these funds to implement sustainable practices, contribute to community development, or engage in socially responsible initiatives.

- **Aligning with Global Trends**: This alignment with social and environmental causes can enhance brand image and appeal to a growing segment of socially-conscious consumers.

5. Providing Access to Resources and Networks

- **Networking Opportunities**: Grants often come with opportunities to connect with mentors, industry leaders, and peer networks, providing valuable insights and opening doors to new possibilities.

- **Skill Development and Support**: Some grant programs offer training, workshops, and support services, which can be instrumental in building the skills and capacities of the business team.

6. Mitigating Financial Risks

- **Reducing Financial Burdens**: By offering non-repayable funding, grants alleviate the pressure of immediate returns on investment, allowing businesses to focus on long-term goals and sustainable growth.

- **Diversifying Funding Sources**: Grants can be a part of a diversified funding strategy, reducing reliance on any single source of capital and thus spreading financial risk.

Grants are a potent tool in the arsenal of business growth strategies. They offer not just financial support but also opportunities for innovation, credibility enhancement, market expansion, social responsibility, networking, skill development, and risk mitigation. Understanding the multifaceted role of grants in business growth is essential for any business looking to leverage this form of funding to its full potential.

Chapter 2: Preparing for Grants

Assessing Your Business Needs

Before diving into the world of grant applications, it is crucial for a business to thoroughly assess its needs and understand how a grant can align with and support its goals. This assessment forms the foundation for identifying the right grant opportunities and crafting effective applications.

1. Identifying Your Objectives

- **Short-term and Long-term Goals**: Begin by outlining your business's immediate and long-term objectives. Are you looking to expand your operations, invest in research and development, or enter new markets?

- **Strategic Alignment**: Ensure that your goals align with your overall business strategy. Grants should support and enhance your strategic direction, not divert from it.

2. Analyzing Your Project Requirements

- **Project Specifics**: Detail the specific projects for which you seek funding. This could include new product development, community initiatives, or infrastructure upgrades.

- **Budget Estimation**: Accurately estimate the budget required for your project. This should include direct costs like materials and labor, as well as indirect costs like overheads.

3. Understanding Your Capability and Capacity

- **Resource Assessment**: Evaluate your current resources, including staff, technology, and facilities. Determine what additional resources will be needed for your project.

- **Capacity for Project Management**: Assess your team's ability to manage and execute the project. Consider factors like expertise, experience, and time availability.

4. Identifying Gaps and Challenges

- **Gap Analysis**: Identify any gaps in your capabilities or resources that need to be addressed to successfully complete the project.

- **Anticipating Challenges**: Consider potential challenges or obstacles that could arise during the project and think about how these could be mitigated.

5. Evaluating Impact and Feasibility

- **Impact Assessment**: Reflect on the potential impact of the project on your business. How will it drive growth, innovation, or competitiveness?

- **Feasibility Study**: Conduct a feasibility study to ensure that the project is viable and sustainable. This should include an analysis of market demand, regulatory environment, and potential risks.

6. Aligning with Grant Opportunities

- **Matching Needs with Grant Criteria**: With a clear understanding of your business needs and project specifics, you can more effectively match these with the criteria and objectives of various grants.

- **Prioritizing Opportunities**: Not all grants will be a perfect fit. Prioritize those opportunities that best align with your business needs and have the greatest potential for success.

Assessing your business needs is a critical step in preparing for grant funding. It involves a deep understanding of your business goals, project requirements, resources, and the potential impact of the project. This thorough assessment not only aids in identifying the most suitable grant opportunities but also lays the groundwork for a compelling grant application.

Identifying Suitable Grants

After assessing your business needs, the next critical step is to identify the grants that are most suitable for your projects and goals. This process involves researching and analyzing various grant opportunities to find those that align best with your business's objectives, capabilities, and needs.

1. Researching Grant Sources

- **Start with Specificity**: Begin your search with grants that specifically target your industry, project type, or business size. This could include grants for technology innovation, small business development, or environmental sustainability.

- **Utilize Online Databases and Resources**: Leverage online grant databases, government websites, and industry-specific resources to find available grants. These platforms often provide comprehensive listings and search tools to filter opportunities by criteria like location, industry, and grant type.

- **Networking and Industry Events**: Attend industry conferences, seminars, and networking events where you can learn about grant opportunities and get insights from peers and experts.

2. Analyzing Grant Requirements and Objectives

- **Eligibility Criteria**: Carefully review the eligibility criteria for each grant. This can include business size, location, type of project, financial status, and more.

- **Grant Objectives**: Understand the objectives of the granting organization. Aligning your project with these objectives is key to a successful application.

- **Funding Scope and Limitations**: Assess the scope of the funding – what it covers and what it does not. Some grants may cover the entire project cost, while others may only fund a portion.

3. Evaluating the Compatibility with Your Business

- **Alignment with Business Goals**: Ensure that the grant aligns with your business goals and strategic direction. The grant should support your project in a way that contributes to your long-term business objectives.

- **Resource and Time Commitment**: Consider the resource and time commitment required for the application process and project execution. Ensure that your business can commit the necessary resources without disrupting its core operations.

4. Prioritizing Potential Grants

- **Assess the Potential Impact**: Evaluate how each grant could impact your business, considering factors like the amount of funding, visibility, and networking opportunities.

- **Success Probability**: Consider your chances of success. Prioritize grants where you have a strong alignment with the criteria and a competitive edge.

- **Application Deadlines and Timelines**: Be mindful of application deadlines and timelines. Planning ahead is crucial to ensure that you have adequate time to prepare a strong application.

5. Creating a Grant Application Plan

- **Shortlist Grants**: Based on your analysis, create a shortlist of the most suitable grants.

- **Develop an Application Timeline**: For each grant on your shortlist, develop a timeline that includes key milestones like gathering necessary information, writing the proposal, and submission deadlines.

Identifying the right grants requires diligent research, careful analysis, and strategic alignment with your business's needs and goals. This process is fundamental to not only enhancing your chances of success but also ensuring that the grant, if secured, will have a meaningful impact on your business. The next steps will involve diving into the specifics of crafting and submitting a winning grant proposal, which we will explore in the following chapters.

Understanding Eligibility Criteria

Understanding and meeting the eligibility criteria is a crucial step in the grant application process. Eligibility criteria are the standards set by grant providers to determine who can apply for and receive funding. These criteria vary widely depending on the grantor and the purpose of the grant.

1. Common Types of Eligibility Criteria

- **Business Type and Size**: Many grants specify the type of business (e.g., for-profit, non-profit) and size (e.g., small, medium-sized) that can apply.

- **Industry or Sector**: Some grants are specific to certain industries or sectors, such as technology, healthcare, education, or environmental sustainability.

- **Geographical Location**: Many grants are limited to businesses operating in a certain region, country, or community.

- **Project-Specific Requirements**: Grants often fund specific types of projects or initiatives. Your project must align with these specified goals, whether they are research, community development, technology innovation, etc.

- **Financial Health**: Certain grants require businesses to demonstrate financial stability or need, while others might require matching funds or co-investment.

- **Previous Grant Awards**: Some grantors restrict eligibility to businesses that have not previously received funding from them, or require a certain period between grants.

2. Researching and Interpreting Criteria

- **Thoroughly Review Grant Announcements**: Grant announcements and calls for applications usually provide detailed eligibility criteria. Read these documents carefully to fully understand the requirements.

- **Seek Clarification if Needed**: If any criteria are unclear, contact the grant provider for clarification. Misunderstanding eligibility criteria can lead to a rejected application.

- **Assess Your Qualification**: Honestly assess whether your business meets all the eligibility criteria. Applying for a grant for which you are ineligible is a waste of time and resources.

3. Documentation and Proof

- **Gather Necessary Documentation**: Prepare to provide documentation that proves your eligibility. This can include business registration documents, financial statements, project plans, and more.

- **Maintain Accurate and Up-to-Date Records**: Ensure that all documentation is accurate, professional, and up-to-date. This not only supports your eligibility but also reflects your business's credibility.

4. Strategic Considerations

- **Aligning with Grant Goals**: Beyond meeting the basic criteria, consider how your project and business align with the broader goals of the grant. This strategic alignment can strengthen your application.

- **Adapting Projects to Fit Criteria**: In some cases, it may be worthwhile to slightly adapt your project to better fit the grant criteria, as long as it remains true to your business's objectives and values.

Understanding and meeting the eligibility criteria are fundamental to a successful grant application. It requires careful analysis, honest assessment, and thorough preparation. By ensuring that your business and project align with these criteria, you significantly increase your chances of not only being eligible to apply but also being successful in your application.

Chapter 3: Researching Grants

How to Find Relevant Grants

Finding relevant grants is a critical step in the grant-seeking process. It involves strategic research to identify funding opportunities that align with your business's needs and objectives. This section offers guidance on how to effectively locate grants that are most suitable for your business.

1. Utilizing Online Grant Databases and Search Tools

- **Government Portals**: Start with government websites, such as [Your Country's] Government Grants portal or the Small Business Administration site, which list various federal and state grant opportunities.

- **Specialized Grant Databases**: Use databases like Grants.gov (U.S.), the Foundation Center, or sector-specific databases that compile grant listings across various fields and industries.

- **Search Filters**: Make use of search filters in these databases to narrow down grant opportunities by industry, grant type, eligibility criteria, and funding amount.

2. Networking and Industry Associations

- **Industry Events and Conferences**: Attend events, workshops, and conferences relevant to your industry. These gatherings can be a source of information about new and upcoming grants.

- **Professional Associations**: Engage with industry associations and groups. These organizations often have insider knowledge about grant opportunities and may offer member-specific grants.

- **Networking with Peers**: Connect with other business owners and professionals in your field. They can provide tips based on their experiences and might alert you to grants you weren't aware of.

3. Subscribing to Newsletters and Publications

- **Industry Publications**: Subscribe to industry journals, magazines, and newsletters. They often feature articles about grant opportunities and funding trends.

- **Grant-specific Newsletters**: Sign up for newsletters from grant databases or funding organizations to receive regular updates on available grants.

4. Following Grant Agencies on Social Media

- **Social Media Channels**: Follow grant agencies, government departments, and industry leaders on social media platforms. They frequently post updates about funding opportunities, deadlines, and workshops.

- **Joining Online Forums and Groups**: Participate in online forums and social media groups focused on business funding. These platforms can be a valuable source of real-time information and advice.

5. Collaborating with Grant Consultants or Writers

- **Professional Assistance**: Consider hiring a grant consultant or writer. These professionals have expertise in identifying a wide range of grant opportunities and can save you time in the research process.

- **Consultation Services**: Even if not hiring for full services, some consultants offer targeted sessions to help identify potential grants for your business.

6. Staying Informed about Government Policies and Initiatives

- **Policy Changes and New Initiatives**: Keep abreast of changes in government policies and new initiatives, as these often lead to the launch of new grant programs.

The process of finding relevant grants requires a multi-faceted approach, combining online research, networking, staying informed through publications and social media, and potentially seeking professional assistance. By casting a wide net and utilizing various resources, you can increase your chances of finding grants that align well with your business's goals and projects.

Utilizing Online Databases and Resources

In today's digital age, online databases and resources are invaluable tools for finding grant opportunities. They provide a centralized platform for searching and identifying grants that match your business's needs. This section will guide you through effectively using these resources to streamline your grant search process.

1. Understanding Online Grant Databases

- **Comprehensive Listings**: Online databases typically offer comprehensive listings of grants from various sources including government, corporate, and non-profit organizations.

- **Search Functionality**: These platforms often have advanced search functionality that allows you to filter grants by criteria such as industry, grant type, location, and funding amount.

2. Key Online Grant Databases

- **Government Grant Portals**: Websites like Grants.gov in the U.S. or [Your Country's Government Grant Portal] offer extensive listings of government-funded grants.

- **Foundation Center**: A resource for finding grants from private foundations and corporate grantmakers.

- **Sector-Specific Databases**: Depending on your industry, there may be databases dedicated to specific sectors, such as technology, healthcare, or environmental grants.

3. Tips for Using Online Databases

- **Regular Checks and Updates**: Grant opportunities are continually being updated. Regularly check databases for new listings and updates to existing grants.

- **Create Alerts**: Many databases allow you to set up alerts based on your search criteria, so you can be notified when new grants that match your preferences are added.

- **Read Descriptions Carefully**: Ensure that you read the grant descriptions carefully to understand the objectives, eligibility criteria, and application requirements.

4. Leveraging Other Online Resources

- **Government Websites**: Beyond databases, government websites often have sections dedicated to business grants and funding opportunities.

- **Industry Association Websites**: Check the websites of industry associations, as they may have listings or information about grants relevant to your sector.

- **Research Reports and Publications**: Keep an eye on industry reports and publications that may discuss funding trends and new grant opportunities.

5. Organizing Your Findings

- **Create a Database**: Maintain a personal database or spreadsheet of potential grants with details like deadlines, eligibility criteria, and application requirements.

- **Prioritization**: Based on your assessment, prioritize the grants in order of relevance and the likelihood of success.

6. Staying Up-to-Date

- **Subscribe to Newsletters**: Many grant databases and industry associations offer newsletters. Subscribe to these to receive regular updates.

- **Participate in Webinars and Workshops**: Attend webinars and workshops offered by grant providers or industry groups. These can provide insights into the application process and new opportunities.

Utilizing online databases and resources is a crucial step in the grant research process. These tools offer a wealth of information and can significantly streamline your search for suitable grants. By actively engaging with these resources, staying organized, and keeping up-to-date, you can effectively identify a range of grant opportunities well-suited to your business's needs.

Networking for Grant Opportunities

Networking is a powerful tool in the grant-seeking process. It involves building and leveraging relationships to uncover and capitalize on grant opportunities. This section explores how effective networking can open doors to funding options that might not be widely advertised and provide valuable insights into the grant application process.

1. Understanding the Value of Networking

- **Access to Insider Knowledge**: Networking can provide access to information about grants that may not be publicly listed or are known only within certain circles.

- **Advice and Guidance**: Experienced professionals in your network can offer advice on grant applications and insights into what funding organizations are looking for.

- **Building Relationships**: Establishing connections with industry peers, grant agencies, and funding bodies can be beneficial for future grant opportunities and collaborations.

2. Strategies for Effective Networking

- **Industry Conferences and Events**: Attend conferences, seminars, and networking events in your industry. These are excellent opportunities to meet people with similar interests and potential contacts in funding organizations.

- **Join Professional Associations**: Become an active member of relevant professional associations. These groups often have resources and networking opportunities focused on grant funding.

- **Engage in Online Communities**: Participate in online forums, LinkedIn groups, or social media networks related to your industry and grant funding.

3. Networking with Grant Providers

- **Attend Grant Information Sessions**: Many grant providers hold information sessions or webinars about their grant programs. Attend these to understand their requirements and make direct contact.

- **Establish Direct Contact**: If possible, establish a direct line of communication with grant agencies. A brief meeting or conversation can provide valuable insights and help your application stand out.

4. Leveraging Existing Contacts

- **Tap into Your Current Network**: Don't overlook your existing contacts. Reach out to colleagues, mentors, and business associates for potential leads or advice.

- **Follow-up and Relationship Building**: After making new contacts, follow up with them. Building a genuine relationship is key to effective networking.

5. Networking Etiquette

- **Be Professional and Prepared**: In all interactions, be professional. Have your business pitch ready, and be clear about what you're looking for.

- **Offer Value in Return**: Networking is a two-way street. Think about how you can offer value to your contacts, whether it's sharing information, resources, or support.

6. Documenting and Following up on Leads

- **Keep Track of Contacts and Information**: Maintain a record of the people you meet and the information you gather. This can be a valuable resource as you apply for grants and in future business endeavors.

- **Regular Follow-ups**: Regularly touch base with your contacts to keep your relationships active and stay on top of new opportunities.

Networking is an essential aspect of researching grant opportunities. It goes beyond merely finding potential grants; it's about building relationships that can provide valuable insights, guidance, and direct leads to funding opportunities. Effective networking involves active participation in relevant events and communities, establishing connections with grant providers, and maintaining these relationships through regular engagement.

Chapter 4: Crafting a Winning Proposal

Key Components of a Grant Proposal

Writing a compelling grant proposal is a critical skill in securing funding for your business. A successful proposal clearly communicates the value of your project, its alignment with the grantor's objectives, and your capability to execute it effectively. This section outlines the essential components of a winning grant proposal.

1. Executive Summary

- **Purpose and Vision**: Begin with a clear and concise statement of your project's purpose. Highlight the vision and the specific issue or opportunity your project addresses.

- **Summary of Request**: Briefly summarize what you are asking for, including the funding amount and how it will be used.

2. Statement of Need

- **Problem Definition**: Clearly define the problem or need your project will address. Provide evidence and data to support the existence and significance of this problem.

- **Target Audience**: Describe who will benefit from the project. Be specific about your target audience or community.

3. Project Description

- **Goals and Objectives**: Outline the primary goals and objectives of your project. These should be specific, measurable, achievable, relevant, and time-bound (SMART).

- **Strategies and Activities**: Detail the strategies and activities you will employ to achieve these objectives. Explain why these approaches were chosen.

- **Innovation and Uniqueness**: If applicable, highlight what makes your project innovative or unique.

4. Budget and Financial Information

- **Detailed Budget**: Present a detailed budget that outlines how the grant funds will be used. Include direct costs (like materials and labor) and indirect costs (like overhead expenses).

- **Financial Need and Justification**: Explain why funding is needed and how it will make a difference in the project's success.

5. Organization Information

- **Background and Capability**: Provide background information about your business, including its history, mission, and past achievements.

- **Management Team**: Introduce the key team members and their qualifications, emphasizing their ability to successfully implement the project.

6. Evaluation Plan

- **Measuring Success**: Describe how you will measure and evaluate the success of the project. Include the metrics and methods you will use.

- **Reporting**: Explain how and when you will report on the project's progress and outcomes to the grantor.

7. Sustainability Plan

- **Long-term Viability**: Outline how the project will be sustained beyond the grant period. This could include plans for future funding, ongoing revenue strategies, or scalability.

8. Conclusion

- **Reiterate the Impact**: Conclude by reiterating the importance and potential impact of the project. Leave the grantor with a clear sense of why your project deserves funding.

9. Appendices and Supporting Documents

- **Additional Information**: Include any additional information or supporting documents that strengthen your proposal. This may include letters of support, endorsements, relevant research, or case studies.

A well-crafted grant proposal is more than just a funding request; it's a comprehensive and persuasive document that showcases your project's value, feasibility, and alignment with the grantor's objectives. By meticulously addressing each of these key components, you significantly enhance your chances of creating a winning proposal.

Writing a Compelling Narrative

The narrative of your grant proposal is where you tell the story of your project and its potential impact. It's crucial to craft a narrative that is not only clear and concise but also engaging and persuasive. This section provides guidance on how to write a narrative that captures the attention of grant reviewers and effectively communicates the value of your project.

1. Start with a Strong Introduction

- **Hook the Reader**: Begin with a compelling statement or story that draws the reader in. This could be a powerful statistic, a brief anecdote, or a vivid description of the problem your project addresses.

- **Set the Scene**: Clearly set the context of your project. Provide background information that helps the reader understand the situation or need.

2. Articulate the Problem or Need

- **Be Specific and Relatable**: Clearly define the problem or need your project addresses. Use specific data, examples, or stories to make it relatable and real to the reader.

- **Show, Don't Just Tell**: Use descriptive language to paint a picture of the issue. This helps to create an emotional connection with the reader.

3. Describe Your Solution

- **Link Solution to Problem**: Clearly explain how your project addresses the identified problem or need. Make a direct connection between the two.

- **Highlight the Benefits**: Focus on the benefits and impact of your solution. Explain how it will improve situations, change lives, or contribute to the field.

4. Showcase Your Capability

- **Demonstrate Expertise and Experience**: Use the narrative to showcase your business's expertise and experience in handling such projects. Mention past successes or relevant expertise.

- **Build Trust**: Provide enough detail to show that you have thoroughly thought through the project and are capable of executing it successfully.

5. Use Persuasive and Engaging Language

- **Be Persuasive**: Write in a way that convinces the reader of the importance and feasibility of your project. Use strong, confident language.

- **Engage the Reader**: Use storytelling techniques to make your narrative engaging. This could include anecdotes, case studies, or testimonials.

6. Keep It Clear and Structured

- **Stay Focused**: Stick to the point and keep your narrative focused on the key elements of your proposal.

- **Logical Flow**: Ensure that your narrative has a logical flow, with each section smoothly leading to the next.

7. Conclude with Impact

- **Summarize Key Points**: Conclude by summarizing the main points of your narrative, reinforcing the importance and impact of your project.

- **End with a Call to Action**: Leave the reader with a clear sense of why action is needed now and why your project is the right solution.

8. Proofread and Edit

- **Clarity and Precision**: Make sure your narrative is clear, precise, and free of jargon.

- **Proofreading**: Carefully proofread your narrative for grammatical errors and clarity. Consider getting an external review for unbiased feedback.

A compelling narrative is the heart of your grant proposal. It brings your project to life and can significantly influence the decision-making process of grant reviewers. By crafting a narrative that is engaging, clear, and persuasive, you greatly enhance your proposal's chances of success.

Budgeting and Financial Planning

A well-prepared budget is a critical component of a grant proposal. It provides a transparent, detailed plan of how you intend to allocate and manage the grant funds. This section will guide you through creating a budget that is both realistic and aligned with the objectives of your project and the grantor.

1. Understanding the Purpose of the Budget

- **Financial Blueprint**: The budget serves as a financial blueprint for your project, outlining all expected costs and how you plan to use the funding.

- **Trust and Credibility**: A clear and detailed budget builds trust with the grantor by demonstrating your business's financial planning capabilities and project management skills.

2. Detailing Direct Costs

- **Project-specific Expenses**: Include all costs directly associated with the project, such as materials, equipment, labor, and travel.

- **Detailed Breakdown**: Provide a detailed breakdown of these costs. For instance, rather than a single figure for 'materials,' itemize it into specific types of materials and their respective costs.

3. Including Indirect Costs

- **Overhead Expenses**: Account for indirect costs, which are not directly attributable to the project but are necessary for its execution, like utilities, rent, or administrative expenses.

- **Percentage Allocation**: These costs can be allocated as a percentage of the total budget, based on standard rates or past organizational budgets.

4. Considering Contingencies

- **Unforeseen Expenses**: Include a contingency fund in your budget for unforeseen expenses. A general rule of thumb is to allocate around 5-10% of the total direct costs for contingencies.

- **Justification**: Provide a rationale for this contingency fund, explaining that it is for unexpected costs that could arise during the project.

5. Demonstrating Cost-effectiveness

- **Competitive Pricing**: Show that you have sought competitive pricing for materials and services to ensure cost-effectiveness.

- **Value for Money**: Demonstrate that every dollar spent contributes to the overall objectives of the project, offering good value for money to the grantor.

6. Aligning Budget with Narrative

- **Consistency**: Ensure that your budget aligns with the narrative of your proposal. Each line item in your budget should have a corresponding element in your project description.

- **Narrative Explanation**: Use the narrative to explain significant budget items, particularly those that might seem unusual or unusually high.

7. Financial Sustainability Post-Grant

- **Long-term Financial Planning**: Outline how the project will be financially sustained after the grant period. This might include plans for revenue generation, future funding, or scaling down costs.

8. Formatting and Presentation

- **Clear and Professional**: Present your budget in a format that is clear, professional, and easy to understand. Use tables and charts where appropriate.

- **Review and Accuracy**: Double-check for mathematical accuracy and ensure that the budget is free from errors.

A well-structured and realistic budget is essential in demonstrating your project's feasibility and your organization's financial acumen. It shows the grantor that you have a clear plan for how their funds will be used effectively and responsibly, increasing the credibility of your proposal.

Chapter 5: The Application Process

Understanding the Application Guidelines

Navigating the application process for a grant begins with a thorough understanding of the application guidelines. These guidelines are the roadmap provided by the grantor, detailing how to submit your proposal, what information to include, and what rules to follow. Adhering closely to these guidelines is crucial for a successful application.

1. Familiarizing Yourself with the Guidelines

- **Read Thoroughly**: Before starting your application, read through all the guidelines provided by the grantor. Pay attention to every detail, as missing even a small requirement can lead to your application being disqualified.

- **Understanding Requirements**: Identify key requirements such as eligibility criteria, submission deadlines, format specifications, required documents, and the scope of projects funded.

2. Identifying Key Components and Deadlines

- **Components of the Application**: Break down the application into its key components. These could include the proposal narrative, budget, project timelines, letters of support, and other required documents.

- **Submission Deadlines**: Note all deadlines, including those for the full proposal, letters of intent (if required), and any other relevant dates. Consider setting internal deadlines ahead of the actual deadlines to ensure timely submission.

3. Comprehending Formatting and Submission Rules

- **Formatting Instructions**: Pay attention to specific formatting instructions such as font size, margin widths, page limits, and document types (e.g., PDF, Word).

- **Submission Method**: Understand the method of submission (e.g., online portal, email, mail) and any technical requirements or constraints associated with it.

4. Clarifying Ambiguities

- **Seek Clarification**: If any aspect of the guidelines is unclear, contact the grantor for clarification. It's better to ask questions than to assume and risk making an error.

- **Use Available Resources**: Many grantors provide FAQs, webinars, or workshops to help applicants understand the application process. Take advantage of these resources.

5. Adapting Your Proposal to Fit the Guidelines

- **Tailoring Your Proposal**: Adapt your proposal to meet the specific criteria and preferences outlined in the guidelines. This includes focusing on the aspects that the grantor emphasizes and adhering to their preferred structure.

- **Compliance Check**: Before submitting, double-check your application against the guidelines to ensure full compliance.

6. Organizing Application Materials

- **Systematic Approach**: Develop a system to organize and track your application materials. This can include a checklist of required documents and a timeline for preparing and submitting each component.

- **Backing Up Work**: Regularly back up your application materials to avoid losing any progress in case of technical issues.

Understanding and following the application guidelines is fundamental to the grant application process. These guidelines are not just a list of rules but a reflection of what the grantor values and expects in a proposal. By meticulously adhering to these guidelines, you significantly increase your chances of submitting a successful and well-received grant application.

Common Mistakes to Avoid

Navigating the grant application process can be challenging, and even small errors can significantly impact the success of your application. Being aware of common pitfalls can help you avoid them. This section highlights typical mistakes applicants make and provides advice on how to steer clear of these errors.

1. Ignoring the Guidelines

- **Mistake**: Overlooking or misinterpreting the application guidelines.

- **Avoidance Strategy**: Read and re-read the guidelines thoroughly. If anything is unclear, seek clarification from the grantor. Use a checklist to ensure all requirements are met.

2. Inadequate Research

- **Mistake**: Applying for grants without sufficient research, leading to misalignment between the project and the grantor's objectives.

- **Avoidance Strategy**: Conduct thorough research to ensure that your project and the grant's goals are well-aligned. Tailor your proposal to reflect this alignment.

3. Procrastination and Late Submissions

- **Mistake**: Waiting until the last minute to start or submit the application, leading to rushed work or missed deadlines.

- **Avoidance Strategy**: Start early and set internal deadlines. Plan for contingencies to avoid last-minute rushes.

4. Unclear or Unfocused Proposals

- **Mistake**: Submitting a proposal that is vague, overly technical, or lacks a clear focus.

- **Avoidance Strategy**: Write a clear, concise, and compelling narrative. Avoid jargon and ensure your objectives and impact are plainly stated.

5. Overlooking Budget Details

- **Mistake**: Presenting an unrealistic, incomplete, or unclear budget.

- **Avoidance Strategy**: Develop a detailed, accurate budget that aligns with the narrative. Clearly justify each expense and ensure the numbers add up correctly.

6. Neglecting the Importance of Sustainability

- **Mistake**: Failing to address how the project will continue or be sustained after the grant period.

- **Avoidance Strategy**: Include a sustainability plan that outlines how the project will continue to operate and be funded in the future.

7. Overpromising and Under-delivering

- **Mistake**: Making unrealistic promises about what the project will achieve.

- **Avoidance Strategy**: Set realistic goals and deliverables. It's better to promise less and overdeliver than to fail to meet overly ambitious expectations.

8. Insufficient Proofreading and Editing

- **Mistake**: Submitting an application with errors, typos, or grammatical issues.

- **Avoidance Strategy**: Thoroughly proofread your application. Consider having it reviewed by a colleague or a professional editor.

9. Failure to Showcase Organizational Strengths and Capabilities

- **Mistake**: Not effectively conveying your organization's strengths and capacity to carry out the project.

- **Avoidance Strategy**: Highlight your team's experience, past successes, and relevant skills. Demonstrate your capability to manage and successfully implement the project.

10. Overlooking Required Attachments and Supporting Documents

- **Mistake**: Forgetting to include all required attachments and supporting documents.

- **Avoidance Strategy**: Double-check the guidelines for required documents. Keep a checklist and ensure all necessary attachments are included before submission.

Avoiding these common mistakes can greatly enhance the quality and effectiveness of your grant application. Paying attention to detail, adhering to guidelines, and presenting a well-thought-out proposal will increase your chances of success and demonstrate your professionalism and commitment to the project.

Tips for a Strong Application

Creating a strong grant application is key to securing funding. It requires careful planning, clear communication, and a strategic approach. This section provides essential tips to enhance the quality and effectiveness of your grant application.

1. Align Your Proposal with the Grantor's Objectives

- **Tip**: Tailor your application to align closely with the grantor's goals and objectives. Demonstrate how your project contributes to their agenda or mission.
- **Strategy**: Research the grantor thoroughly to understand their priorities and tailor your proposal to reflect these.

2. Tell a Compelling Story

- **Tip**: Use your proposal to tell a story that engages the reader. Clearly articulate the problem, your solution, and the potential impact.
- **Strategy**: Use real-world examples, anecdotes, or case studies to make your proposal more relatable and compelling.

3. Be Clear and Concise

- **Tip**: Avoid jargon and technical language. Ensure that your proposal is clear, concise, and easily understandable by a non-specialist.

- **Strategy**: Have someone outside your field review your application to ensure clarity.

4. Provide Detailed, Accurate Budgets

- **Tip**: Include a detailed and realistic budget that aligns with your project plan. Be transparent about how funds will be used.

- **Strategy**: Break down costs into specific categories, and provide justification for each expense.

5. Demonstrate Organizational Capability

- **Tip**: Showcase your organization's experience, expertise, and success in managing similar projects.

- **Strategy**: Highlight past achievements, qualifications of team members, and organizational strengths.

6. Include a Strong Sustainability Plan

- **Tip**: Show how your project will continue to have an impact beyond the grant period.

- **Strategy**: Outline strategies for long-term funding, future scalability, or integration into ongoing programs.

7. Pay Attention to Details

- **Tip**: Carefully follow all application instructions, including formatting and submission guidelines.

- **Strategy**: Create a checklist based on the application guidelines and double-check every requirement.

8. Proofread and Edit Thoroughly

- **Tip**: Ensure your application is free from grammatical errors and typos.

- **Strategy**: Proofread your application multiple times and consider having it reviewed by a professional editor or colleague.

9. Seek Feedback Before Submission

- **Tip**: Get feedback on your draft proposal from colleagues, mentors, or professionals in the field.

- **Strategy**: Use this feedback to refine and strengthen your application.

10. Prepare for Possible Follow-Up

- **Tip**: Be prepared for follow-up questions or requests for additional information.

- **Strategy**: Keep detailed project notes and documents organized and accessible for easy reference.

A strong grant application is the result of meticulous planning, strategic alignment with the grantor's objectives, and clear communication. By following these tips, you enhance not only the quality of your application but also your chances of successfully securing grant funding. Remember, each application is a learning opportunity, regardless of the outcome.

Chapter 6: After the Submission

The Review Process Explained

After submitting a grant proposal, it enters a review process conducted by the funding organization. Understanding this process can help set realistic expectations and prepare you for the steps that follow. This section explains the typical stages and considerations of the grant review process.

1. Initial Screening

- **Overview**: The first stage is an initial screening to ensure that applications meet the basic eligibility criteria and adhere to the guidelines.

- **What to Expect**: If there are any discrepancies or missing components, the application may be rejected at this stage. Make sure your application is complete and follows all instructions.

2. In-depth Review

- **Overview**: Proposals that pass the initial screening are subjected to a more detailed review. This is where the content and quality of your proposal are critically assessed.

- **Criteria**: Reviewers evaluate the proposal based on various criteria, such as the project's feasibility, potential impact, budget accuracy, and alignment with the grantor's objectives.

3. Panel Review or Committee Assessment

- **Overview**: Many grantors use a panel of experts or a committee to review applications. This group collectively evaluates and discusses the merits of each proposal.

- **Considerations**: The panel may look for innovative solutions, sustainability, and overall contribution to the field or community. They may also assess the capability of your organization to successfully execute the project.

4. Scoring and Ranking

- **Overview**: Proposals are often scored based on predefined criteria, and then ranked accordingly.
- **Impact on Decision**: The ranking helps the grantor decide which proposals are most deserving of funding, considering the available budget and the number of grants to be awarded.

5. Due Diligence and Verification

- **Overview**: For proposals that rank highly, the grantor may conduct due diligence, which includes verifying the details provided, checking references, or visiting the organization.
- **Preparation**: Be prepared to provide additional information, facilitate site visits, or engage in interviews during this phase.

6. Final Decision and Notification

- **Overview**: After all reviews and verifications are completed, the grantor makes the final decision on which proposals will be funded.
- **Notification**: Applicants are usually notified of the decision via email or letter. This can include both successful and unsuccessful applicants.

7. Feedback for Unsuccessful Applications

- **Possibility**: Some grantors offer feedback on why a proposal was not selected.
- **Benefit**: If available, this feedback can be invaluable for understanding areas of improvement for future applications.

The review process for grant applications can be rigorous and competitive. Understanding this process helps in setting realistic expectations and preparing for the various stages. Regardless of the outcome, each application is a learning experience that can improve your skills and strategies for future grant opportunities.

Handling Rejections and Feedback

Receiving a rejection for a grant proposal can be disappointing, but it's a common part of the application process. How you handle this rejection and the feedback provided can significantly impact your future success. This section offers guidance on managing rejections constructively and using feedback to improve subsequent applications.

1. Understanding that Rejection is Common

- **Reality Check**: Recognize that grant funding is highly competitive, and rejections are more common than approvals. Being turned down does not necessarily reflect the quality or importance of your proposal.

- **Maintaining Perspective**: View rejection as a normal step in the journey toward securing funding, rather than a reflection of your worth or capabilities.

2. Seeking and Reviewing Feedback

- **Requesting Feedback**: If not provided, request feedback from the grantor on why your proposal was not successful. Most grantors are willing to offer insights to help applicants improve.

- **Analyzing Feedback**: Carefully review the feedback to identify specific areas where your proposal could be strengthened.

3. Responding Professionally to Rejection

- **Professional Attitude**: Respond to the rejection professionally. Thank the grantor for the opportunity and the feedback, and express hope for future collaborations.

- **Building Relationships**: Maintain a positive relationship with the grantor. Showing professionalism in the face of rejection can leave a good impression for future applications.

4. Learning from the Experience

- **Identifying Lessons**: Use the rejection as a learning opportunity. Analyze both your proposal and the feedback to identify key areas for improvement.

- **Consulting with Peers**: Discuss the feedback with colleagues or mentors who can provide an objective perspective and additional advice.

5. Refining Your Proposal for Future Submissions

- **Making Improvements**: Revise your proposal based on the feedback. This might involve clarifying certain sections, providing more detailed information, adjusting your budget, or rethinking your project's scope.

- **Considering Other Opportunities**: Use the revised proposal to apply for other grant opportunities. The improvements made can increase your chances of success with other funders.

6. Staying Motivated and Persistent

- **Maintaining Determination**: Stay motivated despite the setback. Persistence is key in the grant application process.

- **Broadening Your Search**: Continue searching for other grant opportunities. Diversifying your applications can increase your chances of success.

7. Seeking Support and Guidance

- **Professional Advice**: Consider seeking advice from a grant writing professional or attending workshops to enhance your skills.

- **Peer Support**: Engage with peer networks for support, encouragement, and shared experiences.

Handling rejections and feedback with a positive and constructive approach is crucial in the world of grant funding. Use these experiences as stepping stones to refine your proposals and strategies. Remember, every rejection brings you closer to understanding what it takes to craft a successful grant application.

Resubmission Strategies

If your grant proposal was not successful, resubmission can be a viable strategy. Many successful grant applications are the result of refining and resubmitting proposals based on feedback and additional insights. This section outlines strategies for effective resubmission.

1. Analyze the Feedback Thoroughly

- **Understanding Feedback**: Carefully analyze the feedback provided by the grantor. Understand the reasons behind the rejection and identify the key areas for improvement.

- **External Review**: Consider getting an external review of both the feedback and your proposal. A fresh perspective can reveal insights you might have missed.

2. Revise Your Proposal Accordingly

- **Addressing Specific Concerns**: Make revisions directly addressing the grantor's concerns. This could involve more detailed explanations, clearer objectives, a revised budget, or additional supporting data.

- **Improving Clarity and Focus**: Ensure your proposal is clear, focused, and aligns closely with the grantor's objectives and criteria.

3. Update the Proposal with New Data or Developments

- **Incorporate New Information**: If there have been any significant developments or new data since your initial submission, update your proposal to reflect these changes.

- **Strengthening the Proposal**: Use any new achievements, partnerships, or endorsements to strengthen the credibility and appeal of your project.

4. Re-evaluate the Budget

- **Budget Adjustments**: Based on the feedback, adjust your budget to ensure it is realistic, well-justified, and aligns with the project's goals.

- **Cost-effectiveness**: Demonstrate cost-effectiveness and value for money in your revised budget.

5. Consider Timing and Changes in Funding Priorities

- **Reassessment of Timing**: Consider the timing of your resubmission. Sometimes, waiting for a more opportune moment or a change in funding priorities can improve your chances.

- **Stay Informed**: Keep informed about any changes in the grantor's priorities or guidelines that might affect your resubmission.

6. Craft a Cover Letter for Resubmission

- **Acknowledging Past Submission**: Write a cover letter that acknowledges your previous submission and thanks the grantor for their feedback.

- **Highlighting Changes**: Clearly highlight the changes and improvements made in the resubmitted proposal.

7. Maintain Persistence and Optimism

- **Persistence Pays Off**: Understand that securing grant funding often requires persistence. Don't be discouraged by initial rejections.

- **Optimistic Outlook**: Maintain a positive and optimistic attitude. Each submission is a step forward in refining your proposal and understanding the grantor's needs.

8. Expand Your Options

- **Other Funding Sources**: While preparing for resubmission, also look for other potential grant opportunities where your revised proposal might be a good fit.

- **Diversifying Applications**: Applying to multiple sources can increase your chances of securing funding.

Resubmitting a grant proposal is an opportunity to refine and strengthen your application based on valuable feedback and additional insights. It demonstrates your commitment to the project and your willingness to adapt and improve. With a strategic approach to resubmission, your proposal stands a better chance of success in the competitive world of grant funding.

Chapter 7: Managing Grant Funds

Effective Fund Management Strategies

Securing a grant is just the beginning; the real challenge lies in effectively managing the funds to ensure the success of your project and compliance with the grantor's terms. This section discusses strategies for efficient and responsible management of grant funds.

1. Develop a Detailed Financial Plan

- **Budget Adherence**: Create a detailed financial plan that aligns with your original budget proposal. Stick to this budget unless changes are approved by the grantor.

- **Track Expenditures**: Establish a system to track all expenditures against the budget. This will help in maintaining transparency and accountability.

2. Set Up a Separate Accounting System

- **Dedicated Account**: Consider setting up a separate bank account for the grant funds to avoid co-mingling with other funds.

- **Accurate Record-Keeping**: Keep accurate and detailed financial records. Use accounting software that can categorize and track grant-related transactions separately.

3. Regular Monitoring and Reporting

- **Frequent Reviews**: Regularly review your financial status against the project's progress. This helps in identifying any discrepancies or areas where adjustments are needed.

- **Reporting Requirements**: Adhere to the grantor's reporting requirements. Prepare and submit financial reports as outlined in the grant agreement.

4. Ensure Compliance with Grant Terms

- **Understanding Terms**: Be thoroughly familiar with the terms and conditions of the grant, especially regarding the use of funds.

- **Compliance Checks**: Periodically check to ensure that fund usage is in compliance with these terms. Non-compliance can lead to penalties or revocation of the grant.

5. Manage Cash Flow Effectively

- **Cash Flow Planning**: Anticipate and plan for cash flow needs throughout the project. This includes timing of expenditures and understanding how the grantor disburses funds.

- **Reserve Funds**: Maintain a reserve for unexpected costs or delays, within the confines of the grant's terms.

6. Collaboration with Project Team

- **Communication**: Keep open lines of communication with your project team regarding the budget and any financial constraints.

- **Team Involvement**: Involve your team in financial planning and monitoring to ensure that everyone is aware of the budgetary limitations and requirements.

7. Plan for Sustainability Post-Grant

- **Future Funding**: Start planning for financial sustainability post-grant. This might involve securing additional funding, reducing costs, or finding revenue-generating avenues for the project.

8. Conduct Internal Audits

- **Regular Audits**: Conduct regular internal audits to ensure that financial management practices are in line with both your organization's policies and the grantor's requirements.

- **Addressing Issues**: Use audit findings to address and rectify any issues promptly.

9. Seek Professional Advice

- **Financial Expertise**: Don't hesitate to seek advice from financial experts or accountants, especially for larger or more complex grants.

Effective fund management is critical in ensuring the success of your project and maintaining a good relationship with the grantor. It requires careful planning, diligent tracking, and compliance with the grant terms. By implementing these strategies, you can efficiently manage the grant funds and lay a strong foundation for the successful completion of your project.

Reporting and Compliance

Effective management of grant funds extends beyond just financial stewardship; it also involves adhering to reporting requirements and maintaining compliance with the grantor's guidelines. This section focuses on strategies for successful reporting and compliance throughout the grant period.

1. Understanding Reporting Requirements

- **Review Requirements**: Familiarize yourself thoroughly with the reporting requirements outlined in the grant agreement. This includes the frequency of reports, specific data or metrics required, and format guidelines.

- **Prepare in Advance**: Don't wait until the report due date is near. Begin preparing your report well in advance to ensure that it is comprehensive and well-crafted.

2. Maintaining Accurate and Timely Records

- **Detailed Documentation**: Keep detailed records of all activities, expenditures, and outcomes related to the grant. This makes it easier to compile accurate reports.

- **Timely Record-Keeping**: Update your records regularly. Delayed or rushed record-keeping can lead to errors or omissions in reporting.

3. Demonstrating Transparency and Accountability

- **Clear and Honest Reporting**: Be transparent in your reports. If there have been challenges or deviations from the plan, report them honestly and explain the reasons and remedial actions taken.

- **Accountability for Funds**: Show clear accountability for how the funds have been used. Include detailed financial statements and receipts where required.

4. Reporting on Progress and Impact

- **Measure Against Objectives**: In your reports, measure the project's progress against the stated objectives and goals. Use quantifiable metrics where possible.

- **Highlighting Impact**: Emphasize the impact of the project, particularly how it aligns with the grantor's objectives and the broader benefit to the community or field.

5. Compliance with Grant Terms and Conditions

- **Adherence to Terms**: Ensure that all project activities and fund usage comply with the terms and conditions of the grant.

- **Regular Compliance Checks**: Conduct regular checks to ensure ongoing compliance. Address any issues of non-compliance immediately.

6. Communication with the Grantor

- **Open Dialogue**: Maintain open communication with the grantor. If there are significant issues or changes in the project, inform the grantor as soon as possible.

- **Seek Clarifications**: If you are unsure about reporting procedures or compliance issues, seek clarification from the grantor.

7. Preparing for Audits

- **Audit Readiness**: Be prepared for potential audits by the grantor. Ensure all documents and records are in order and easily accessible.

- **Internal Reviews**: Conduct internal reviews or audits to ensure everything is in compliance before submitting reports.

8. Utilizing Reporting as a Tool for Reflection and Planning

- **Reflect on Progress**: Use the reporting process as an opportunity to reflect on the project's progress and challenges.

- **Future Planning**: Assess what has been learned and how it can be applied to future activities and grant applications.

Effective reporting and compliance are crucial aspects of grant fund management. They demonstrate your commitment to the project's success and your accountability to the grantor. Through meticulous record-keeping, transparent reporting, and adherence to grant terms, you can build a strong foundation for both current and future grant endeavors.

Maximizing the Impact of the Grant

Securing a grant is a significant achievement, but the true measure of success lies in how effectively the grant is utilized to maximize its impact. This section offers strategies to ensure that the grant contributes meaningfully to your project's goals and creates a lasting positive effect.

1. Strategic Allocation of Funds

- **Prioritize Key Activities**: Allocate funds to the most critical activities that drive your project forward and align with the grant's objectives.

- **Efficient Use of Resources**: Ensure that every dollar spent contributes to the project's success. Avoid unnecessary expenses and seek cost-effective solutions.

2. Enhancing Project Visibility

- **Promotion and Outreach**: Use a portion of the grant to promote your project. This can include marketing, community engagement, or public relations activities.

- **Showcasing Success**: Share your project's progress and successes through social media, press releases, and presentations to stakeholders.

3. Fostering Partnerships and Collaboration

- **Collaborate with Others**: Look for opportunities to collaborate with other organizations, businesses, or community groups. Partnerships can extend the reach and impact of your project.

- **Leverage Expertise**: Utilize the expertise of partners to enhance project outcomes. This can also lead to resource sharing, reducing overall costs.

4. Building Capacity for Long-Term Impact

- **Invest in Training and Development**: Use grant funds to build the capacity of your team through training, workshops, or hiring skilled personnel.

- **Sustainable Practices**: Implement practices that ensure the project's sustainability beyond the grant period, like developing revenue-generating models or securing additional funding sources.

5. Monitoring and Evaluating Impact

- **Regular Monitoring**: Continuously monitor the project's progress against set goals and objectives. Use this data to make informed decisions and adjustments.

- **Impact Evaluation**: Conduct evaluations to assess the impact of the project. Use both qualitative and quantitative methods to get a comprehensive view.

6. Reporting Impact to Stakeholders

- **Transparent Reporting**: Regularly report the project's impact to stakeholders, including the grantor, your team, and the community. Highlight both achievements and challenges.

- **Engaging Stakeholders**: Keep stakeholders engaged and informed. Their support can be crucial for the project's success and future opportunities.

7. Learning and Adapting for Future Grants

- **Reflect on Lessons Learned**: After the project, reflect on what worked well and what could be improved. Document these lessons for future reference.

- **Adapting Strategies**: Use these insights to adapt your strategies for future grant applications and project management.

Maximizing the impact of a grant requires thoughtful planning, strategic allocation of resources, and continuous monitoring and evaluation. By effectively leveraging the grant, you not only achieve your project's goals but also position your organization for future success and further funding opportunities.

Chapter 8: Success Stories and Case Studies

Interviews with Successful Grantees

Interview 1: Tech Startup CEO - Innovation Grant Success

- **Background**: CEO of a tech startup that received a government innovation grant for developing eco-friendly technology.

- **Key Insights**:

    - **Application Strategy**: Emphasized a strong alignment between the technology's environmental benefits and the grant's focus on sustainability.

    - **Challenges**: Managing the detailed documentation and specific milestones required by the grantor.

    - **Advice**: Highlight the societal impact of your project, not just the commercial benefits.

Interview 2: Non-Profit Director - Community Development Grant

- **Background**: Director of a non-profit that secured a corporate grant for a community development project.

- **Key Insights**:

    - **Finding the Right Fit**: Chose a corporate grantor whose CSR goals closely matched their project's mission.

    - **Fund Management**: Stressed transparent financial practices and regular reporting to maintain trust with the grantor.

    - **Advice**: Build a narrative in your proposal that resonates emotionally and aligns with the grantor's values.

Interview 3: Researcher - Academic Grant Triumph

- **Background**: Lead researcher at a university who won a government grant for scientific research.
- **Key Insights**:
  - **Proposal Writing**: Focused on clearly explaining complex scientific concepts and their potential impact.
  - **Collaboration**: Partnered with other departments to strengthen the proposal's interdisciplinary appeal.
  - **Advice**: Tailor your proposal's language to suit the grantor's expertise level; avoid jargon.

Interview 4: Small Business Owner - Expansion Grant

- **Background**: Owner of a small business that received a local government grant to expand operations.
- **Key Insights**:
  - **Local Focus**: Demonstrated how the business's expansion would benefit the local community and economy.
  - **Budgeting**: Prepared a detailed budget plan to justify the funding amount requested.
  - **Advice**: Leverage your understanding of local needs and how your business meets them.

Interview 5: Arts Organization Founder - Cultural Grant Achievement

- **Background**: Founder of an arts organization that successfully applied for a non-profit foundation grant for a cultural project.
- **Key Insights**:
  - **Community Engagement**: Emphasized the project's role in enriching the local cultural scene and engaging diverse communities.
  - **Sustainability Plan**: Presented a plan for how the project would continue after the grant period.

- **Advice**: Show the broader cultural impact of your project and plan for its long-term viability.

Analysis of Successful Proposals

Understanding what makes a grant proposal successful is key to crafting your own effective applications. This section delves into the analysis of successful proposals, identifying common elements and strategies that contributed to their success.

1. Clear and Compelling Objective

- **Observation**: Successful proposals have a clear, compelling objective that directly aligns with the grantor's mission or goals.
- **Key Takeaway**: Articulate your project's objectives in a way that resonates with the grantor's priorities.

2. Detailed and Realistic Budget

- **Observation**: All successful proposals include a well-structured, detailed, and realistic budget that aligns with the project plan.
- **Key Takeaway**: Ensure that your budget is thorough and reflects a clear understanding of the project's financial needs.

3. Demonstrated Need or Problem Statement

- **Observation**: Successful proposals effectively demonstrate the need or problem they aim to address, supported by data or research.
- **Key Takeaway**: Use data, research, and compelling narratives to illustrate the importance and urgency of the problem your project addresses.

4. Feasibility and Sustainability

- **Observation**: These proposals convincingly outline the feasibility of the project and its sustainability beyond the grant period.
- **Key Takeaway**: Provide a clear plan showing how the project will be implemented successfully and sustained in the future.

5. Strong Organizational Capability

- **Observation**: Proposals that succeed showcase the organization's capability and track record in managing similar projects or initiatives.

- **Key Takeaway**: Highlight your organization's experience, expertise, and past successes relevant to the proposed project.

6. Impact and Evaluation Metrics

- **Observation**: Successful proposals include clear metrics for evaluating the project's impact and effectiveness.

- **Key Takeaway**: Define clear, measurable outcomes for your project and explain how you will evaluate its success.

7. Innovation and Creativity

- **Observation**: Many winning proposals offer innovative solutions or creative approaches to addressing the identified problem.

- **Key Takeaway**: Emphasize any innovative or unique aspects of your project that set it apart from typical approaches.

8. Clarity and Coherence

- **Observation**: Clarity and coherence in writing and presentation are common traits of successful proposals.

- **Key Takeaway**: Ensure your proposal is well-organized, clearly written, and free of jargon or technical terms that could confuse non-expert reviewers.

9. Compliance with Guidelines

- **Observation**: Adherence to the grantor's guidelines is a must in all successful proposals.

- **Key Takeaway**: Follow the application guidelines meticulously, including format, length, and submission procedures.

Analyzing successful grant proposals reveals a pattern of clear objectives, detailed planning, organizational capability, and alignment with grantor's goals. By incorporating these elements into your proposals, you can increase your chances of success in the competitive grant funding landscape.

Lessons Learned

Reflecting on the experiences and insights gained from successful grantees can provide valuable lessons for others embarking on the grant application journey. This section distills the key lessons learned from the case studies and interviews presented earlier in the chapter.

1. Thorough Preparation is Crucial

- **Lesson**: The importance of comprehensive preparation cannot be overstated. Successful grantees spent significant time researching grant opportunities, understanding the grantor's priorities, and tailoring their proposals accordingly.

- **Takeaway**: Invest ample time in preparation before writing your proposal. Understand the grantor's mission and align your project with their objectives.

2. Clarity and Precision Matter

- **Lesson**: Clarity in expressing the project goals, plans, and expected outcomes was a common factor in successful proposals. Precise language and a well-structured narrative made these proposals stand out.

- **Takeaway**: Be clear and concise in your proposal. Avoid jargon and ensure your objectives and methods are easily understandable.

3. Budget Accuracy and Justification Are Key

- **Lesson**: A well-planned, accurately calculated, and properly justified budget was pivotal. Successful grantees demonstrated a clear understanding of their financial needs and how every dollar would be spent.

- **Takeaway**: Develop a detailed budget and justify each expense. Ensure the budget aligns seamlessly with your project plan.

4. Demonstrating Organizational Capacity

- **Lesson**: Grantors are more inclined to fund organizations that demonstrate strong capacity to execute the proposed project. This includes evidence of past successes, relevant experience, and qualified personnel.
- **Takeaway**: Showcase your organization's strengths and past achievements. Highlight the expertise and experience of your team.

5. The Impact Beyond Just Funding

- **Lesson**: Successful grantees viewed the grant not just as a source of funding, but as a means to achieve broader impact, be it social, environmental, or economic.
- **Takeaway**: Emphasize the wider impact of your project. How does it contribute to the community, industry, or a larger cause?

6. Flexibility and Adaptability

- **Lesson**: The ability to adapt to unforeseen challenges and to revise plans as needed was crucial for many successful projects.
- **Takeaway**: Be prepared to adapt your project as it progresses. Flexibility can be as important as thorough planning.

7. The Value of Feedback and Resilience

- **Lesson**: Many successful applicants had previously faced rejections. They used feedback from these rejections to improve their proposals and approaches.
- **Takeaway**: Treat rejections as learning opportunities. Use feedback constructively to enhance future applications.

8. Building Relationships with Grantors

- **Lesson**: Successful grantees often emphasized the importance of building and maintaining good relationships with grantors, which helped in future funding endeavors.
- **Takeaway**: View your relationship with grantors as a long-term partnership. Communicate effectively and maintain a positive rapport.

The journey to securing and effectively utilizing grant funding is filled with learning opportunities. These lessons, distilled from the experiences of successful grantees, provide a roadmap for others to enhance their grant-seeking strategies and increase their chances of success.

Chapter 9: Advanced Strategies

Building Long-term Relationships with Funders

Securing a grant is often the beginning of a valuable relationship with a funder. Nurturing this relationship can lead to ongoing support, future funding, and collaborative opportunities. This section explores strategies for building and maintaining long-term relationships with grant funders.

1. Understand the Funder's Goals and Values

- **Key Strategy**: Deepen your understanding of the funder's long-term goals, mission, and values. Aligning your projects and communication with these elements shows that you are a partner in their mission.

- **Action Steps**: Attend funder events, read their publications, and engage with their initiatives to gain insights into their overarching goals.

2. Consistent and Open Communication

- **Key Strategy**: Maintain regular communication with your funders, keeping them updated about project progress, successes, and challenges.

- **Action Steps**: Schedule regular updates, share reports, and invite funders to events related to the project. Transparency, especially in times of challenge, builds trust.

3. Delivering on Promises

- **Key Strategy**: Ensure that you meet or exceed the expectations set in your grant proposal. Delivering on your promises reinforces your reliability and credibility.

- **Action Steps**: Stick to your project plan, meet deadlines, and achieve the outlined objectives. If deviations are necessary, communicate these proactively.

4. Showcasing Impact

- **Key Strategy**: Clearly demonstrate the impact of the funder's investment. Tangible results and success stories can validate the funder's decision to support your project.

- **Action Steps**: Collect data, stories, and testimonials that show the impact of your work. Share these success stories with your funder.

5. Expressing Gratitude

- **Key Strategy**: Regularly express gratitude for the support you've received. Recognition of the funder's contribution can strengthen the relationship.

- **Action Steps**: Send thank you notes, acknowledge the funder in public forums, and give them credit in any publications or presentations related to the project.

6. Seeking Feedback and Collaboration

- **Key Strategy**: Actively seek feedback from your funders and be open to collaboration. This can lead to improvements in your project and deepen the relationship.

- **Action Steps**: Invite feedback during meetings or through surveys, and be open to collaborative opportunities that align with your mission.

7. Inviting Funders to Participate

- **Key Strategy**: Invite funders to engage with your project more directly, such as site visits, events, or as part of advisory committees.

- **Action Steps**: Create opportunities for funders to see their impact first-hand and engage with the work they are supporting.

8. Building a Network of Support

- **Key Strategy**: Leverage the relationship to build a broader network of support. Funders can introduce you to other potential donors, partners, or resources.

- **Action Steps**: Engage in networking events hosted by the funder and express interest in meeting other stakeholders in their network.

Building long-term relationships with funders goes beyond the financial aspect; it's about creating a partnership based on shared goals, trust, and mutual benefit. By actively working to strengthen these relationships, your organization can secure a more stable and supportive funding base for future endeavors.

Leveraging Grants for Further Funding

Successfully securing a grant can be a springboard for obtaining additional funding. Grants can enhance your credibility and attract more investors or donors. This section explores how to leverage your grant success to open doors to further funding opportunities.

1. Use Grants as a Seal of Approval

- **Key Strategy**: Treat your grant as a seal of approval or endorsement from the grantor. It demonstrates trust and confidence in your project or organization.

- **Action Steps**: Highlight the grant in your communications and marketing materials. Mention it in pitches, proposals, and meetings with potential investors or donors.

2. Attracting Additional Investors

- **Key Strategy**: Use the grant to attract additional investors. The grant can serve as evidence of the viability and potential of your project.

- **Action Steps**: When approaching new investors, use the grant as a proof point. Show how it validates your project's potential and aligns with market needs.

3. Building Credibility for Crowdfunding

- **Key Strategy**: Leverage the credibility gained from the grant to enhance crowdfunding campaigns.

- **Action Steps**: In your crowdfunding pitch, mention the grant to build trust with potential backers. Use it to show that established organizations believe in your project.

4. Enhancing Grant Applications

- **Key Strategy**: Use previous grant successes to strengthen future grant applications.

- **Action Steps**: In new grant applications, reference past grants as evidence of your ability to successfully manage and complete funded projects.

5. Creating Partnerships and Collaborations

- **Key Strategy**: Utilize the grant as a platform for establishing partnerships and collaborations with other organizations.

- **Action Steps**: Approach potential partners with your grant success story. It can serve as a compelling reason for others to collaborate with you.

6. Networking and Visibility

- **Key Strategy**: Increase your visibility and expand your network as a result of the grant.

- **Action Steps**: Attend and participate in events related to your grantor or industry. Use these opportunities to network and share your success story.

7. Case Studies and Success Stories

- **Key Strategy**: Develop detailed case studies or success stories about what you achieved with the grant.

- **Action Steps**: Share these success stories through your website, social media, and in discussions with potential funders to illustrate the impact of your work.

8. Seeking Follow-On Funding

- **Key Strategy**: Approach the original grantor or similar organizations for follow-on funding, especially if your project has scalable aspects or phases.

- **Action Steps**: Present the results and impacts of your current project, along with a plan for its expansion or next phase, to secure additional funding.

Leveraging a grant successfully for further funding is about showcasing the confidence placed in your project by the grantor and using it as a foundation to build more support. It involves strategic communication, networking, and using your success to attract additional investment and partnerships.

The Role of Partnerships and Collaborations

In the realm of grant funding, partnerships and collaborations can play a pivotal role in enhancing project effectiveness, expanding impact, and even increasing the chances of securing funding. This section explores the strategic importance of partnerships and collaborations in the context of grant-funded projects.

1. Strengthening Grant Proposals

- **Key Strategy**: Collaborations can strengthen grant proposals by pooling expertise, resources, and networks. A partnership can demonstrate to grantors that your project has broader support and capability.

- **Action Steps**: Identify potential partners with complementary skills or resources. Include details of these partnerships in your grant proposals to showcase added strength and capacity.

2. Expanding Project Scope and Impact

- **Key Strategy**: Use partnerships to broaden the scope and impact of your project. Collaborative efforts can address more comprehensive needs and reach wider audiences.

- **Action Steps**: Work with partners to integrate and align your goals, creating a more expansive and impactful project plan.

3. Sharing Resources and Reducing Costs

- **Key Strategy**: Collaborations can lead to sharing of resources, thus reducing costs and optimizing the use of grant funds.

- **Action Steps**: Negotiate resource sharing with partners, such as shared workspaces, joint marketing efforts, or pooled expertise, to maximize the grant's effectiveness.

4. Accessing Additional Expertise and Networks

- **Key Strategy**: Partners can bring additional expertise, experience, and networks, which can be crucial for the project's success.

- **Action Steps**: Leverage the skills, experiences, and contacts of your partners to enhance your project's development and outreach.

5. Enhancing Credibility and Trust

- **Key Strategy**: Collaborating with established organizations or entities can enhance the credibility and trustworthiness of your project in the eyes of funders and stakeholders.

- **Action Steps**: Highlight the track record and reputation of your partners in proposals and communications to bolster your project's credibility.

6. Facilitating Knowledge Exchange and Learning

- **Key Strategy**: Partnerships offer opportunities for knowledge exchange and learning, fostering innovation and continuous improvement in project implementation.

- **Action Steps**: Engage in regular meetings and workshops with partners to exchange ideas, challenges, and best practices.

7. Building Long-Term Support Networks

- **Key Strategy**: Develop long-term relationships with partners for ongoing support and future collaborative opportunities.

- **Action Steps**: Maintain regular communication with partners even after project completion and explore ways to continue the relationship for future initiatives.

8. Navigating Complex Projects

- **Key Strategy**: In complex or large-scale projects, partnerships can facilitate more effective navigation of challenges and increase project resilience.

- **Action Steps**: Divide project responsibilities among partners according to their strengths to ensure efficient project management.

Partnerships and collaborations can significantly enhance the quality and impact of grant-funded projects. They bring additional resources, expertise, and credibility, which not only strengthen your grant proposals but also improve project implementation and outcomes. Strategic collaborations can be a key factor in achieving long-term success and sustainability in grant-funded endeavors.

Chapter 10: The Future of Grant Funding

Emerging Trends in Grant Funding

The landscape of grant funding is continually evolving, shaped by economic, technological, and societal changes. Understanding these trends can help businesses and organizations better prepare and adapt their strategies for future grant opportunities. This section explores the emerging trends in the world of grant funding.

1. Increased Focus on Social Impact and Sustainability

- **Trend Overview**: There's a growing emphasis on projects that demonstrate clear social impact, sustainability, and contributions to community welfare.

- **Implication**: Grant seekers should focus on developing projects that address societal challenges, environmental issues, or promote sustainability.

2. The Rise of Technology and Data-Driven Approaches

- **Trend Overview**: The use of technology and data analytics in both the application and execution of grant-funded projects is increasing.

- **Implication**: Incorporate technology to enhance project efficiency and impact. Utilize data analytics for measuring outcomes and reporting.

3. Collaboration and Partnership Grants

- **Trend Overview**: There is a trend towards funding collaborative projects involving multiple organizations or cross-sector partnerships.

- **Implication**: Seek opportunities for collaboration and partnerships to enhance the appeal and scope of your grant proposals.

4. Diversification of Funding Sources

- **Trend Overview**: Beyond traditional government and foundational grants, there is a rise in corporate grants and alternative funding platforms such as crowdfunding.

- **Implication**: Broaden your search for funding sources. Consider corporate grants and crowdfunding as viable options.

5. Flexibility and Adaptability in Projects

- **Trend Overview**: Grantors are increasingly valuing flexibility and adaptability in projects, especially in response to global challenges like pandemics or climate change.

- **Implication**: Design projects that are adaptable to changing circumstances and can pivot as needed.

6. Emphasis on Localized Grants

- **Trend Overview**: There's a growing focus on localized grant making, targeting specific communities or regions.

- **Implication**: Tailor your proposals to address local issues or needs if applying for these grants. Show an understanding of the local context.

7. Streamlined Application Processes

- **Trend Overview**: Efforts are being made to streamline grant application processes, making them more accessible and less cumbersome.

- **Implication**: Stay updated on changes in application processes and leverage any new tools or platforms that simplify the application process.

8. Enhanced Transparency and Accountability

- **Trend Overview**: Grantors are demanding greater transparency and accountability in how funds are utilized.

- **Implication**: Ensure meticulous record-keeping and reporting. Be prepared to demonstrate the impact of your project clearly.

Staying abreast of these emerging trends in grant funding can provide valuable insights into how the landscape is changing. By understanding and adapting to these trends, grant seekers can enhance their strategies and increase their chances of securing funding in the future.

The Impact of Technology on Grant Seeking

Technology is rapidly transforming the grant seeking process, making it more accessible, efficient, and data-driven. Understanding the influence of technology is crucial for modern grant seekers. This section explores how technology is reshaping the landscape of grant funding.

1. Digital Platforms and Databases

- **Trend Overview**: The emergence of online platforms and databases has revolutionized the way grant seekers find and apply for funding.

- **Implication**: Utilize these digital resources for research and to find grant opportunities that align with your project. Platforms like Grants.gov and Foundation Directory Online are key tools.

2. Automation and Streamlining of Applications

- **Trend Overview**: Many grantors are adopting automated systems for application submissions, which streamlines the process and reduces manual errors.

- **Implication**: Familiarize yourself with these systems and take advantage of their efficiency. Ensure that your applications are formatted correctly for automated processing.

3. Enhanced Communication and Collaboration Tools

- **Trend Overview**: Technology facilitates better communication and collaboration, both internally for project teams and externally with grantors.

- **Implication**: Leverage collaboration tools like project management software and communication platforms to coordinate effectively on grant applications.

4. Data Analytics for Impact Measurement

- **Trend Overview**: Advanced data analytics tools are becoming essential in measuring and reporting the impact of grant-funded projects.

- **Implication**: Invest in data collection and analytics tools to track project progress and outcomes. Use this data to demonstrate impact in reports to funders.

5. Social Media for Outreach and Engagement

- **Trend Overview**: Social media platforms are increasingly used for grant seeking, from discovering opportunities to engaging with funders and promoting projects.

- **Implication**: Maintain an active social media presence to network, discover new grant opportunities, and showcase your project's progress and impact.

6. Crowdfunding as an Alternative Funding Source

- **Trend Overview**: Crowdfunding platforms have emerged as a significant alternative or supplementary funding source for many projects.

- **Implication**: Consider using crowdfunding platforms to supplement your grant funding, especially for projects that resonate with the public.

7. Mobile Accessibility

- **Trend Overview**: The increasing use of mobile devices has made grant seeking more accessible, allowing users to search for grants, submit applications, and communicate on the go.

- **Implication**: Ensure that your digital content, including applications and project updates, is mobile-friendly.

8. AI and Machine Learning

- **Trend Overview**: Artificial intelligence and machine learning are beginning to play a role in predicting funding trends and identifying suitable grants.

- **Implication**: Stay informed about AI tools that can analyze your project's suitability for different grants and predict success rates.

Technology is a powerful tool in the grant seeking process, offering new opportunities and efficiencies. By embracing these technological advances, grant seekers can streamline their search and application processes, enhance communication, and effectively measure and showcase the impact of their projects.

Predictions for the Business Grant Landscape

As we look towards the future, the landscape of business grant funding is likely to evolve in response to global economic trends, technological advancements, and shifting societal priorities. Here are some predictions for how the business grant landscape may change in the coming years.

1. Increased Focus on Sustainable and Social Enterprises

- **Prediction**: There will likely be a surge in grants targeting businesses that contribute to sustainability, social justice, and community development.

- **Implication for Businesses**: Consider incorporating sustainable practices and social impact initiatives into your business model to align with these emerging funding priorities.

2. Greater Integration of Technology in Grant Management

- **Prediction**: The use of technology in grant management, from application to execution and reporting, is expected to become more sophisticated and pervasive.

- **Implication for Businesses**: Stay abreast of digital tools and platforms that can streamline the grant application process and enhance project management efficiency.

3. Shift Towards Flexible and Adaptive Funding Models

- **Prediction**: In response to dynamic global challenges, grant funding may become more flexible, with a focus on adaptability and resilience.

- **Implication for Businesses**: Be prepared to demonstrate flexibility and adaptability in your projects and business plans to cater to these evolving funding models.

4. Emphasis on Collaborative and Multi-sector Partnerships

- **Prediction**: There will likely be an increased emphasis on collaborative grants that encourage partnerships across different sectors, such as public-private partnerships.

- **Implication for Businesses**: Look for opportunities to collaborate with other organizations, including non-profits, academic institutions, and government agencies.

5. Rise in Decentralized and Grassroots Funding

- **Prediction**: We may see a rise in decentralized funding sources, including local grants and community-driven funding initiatives.

- **Implication for Businesses**: Pay attention to local and community-level grant opportunities, which may offer more accessible funding options with less competition.

6. Growing Importance of Data and Impact Measurement

- **Prediction**: Demonstrating measurable impact will become increasingly important in securing business grants.

- **Implication for Businesses**: Invest in robust data collection and impact measurement tools to provide concrete evidence of your project's success and impact.

7. Expansion of International and Cross-border Grant Opportunities

- **Prediction**: There may be an increase in international grant opportunities as businesses become more globally interconnected.

- **Implication for Businesses**: Consider expanding your search to include international grant opportunities, particularly those that align with your business's global objectives or markets.

The future of business grant funding is poised for significant changes, influenced by broader economic, technological, and societal shifts. Staying informed about these trends and adapting your strategies accordingly can position your business to successfully navigate and capitalize on the evolving grant landscape.

Appendices

Glossary of Grant Terms

This glossary provides definitions of common terms used in the grant funding process. Understanding these terms is essential for navigating the world of grant funding effectively.

1. Award Letter: A document sent by the grantor to the grantee formally announcing the approval of the grant application and detailing the terms of the grant.

2. Budget Justification: A detailed description of the estimated costs associated with the grant project, explaining why each cost is necessary.

3. Capacity Building: Efforts or initiatives within an organization aimed at developing its effectiveness and sustainability, often through improvements in management, infrastructure, and operations.

4. Challenge Grant: A grant that provides funds based on the recipient's ability to raise additional funds from other sources.

5. Direct Costs: Costs that are directly attributable to the project, such as salaries for project staff, equipment, and materials.

6. Fiscal Sponsor: An organization that provides fiduciary oversight, financial management, and other administrative services to help build the capacity of charitable projects.

7. Grant Agreement: A formal contract between the grantor and grantee outlining the terms and conditions of the grant.

8. Indirect Costs (Overheads): Expenses not directly tied to the project but necessary for the general operation of the organization, such as utilities, rent, and administrative salaries.

9. In-Kind Contribution: A contribution of goods or services other than money, such as equipment, space, or volunteer time.

10. Matching Funds: Funds that are required to be matched by the grantee, often as a percentage of the grant amount, from other sources.

11. Narrative Report: A report that provides a detailed account of the activities, outcomes, and impact of a grant-funded project.

12. Notice of Award (NOA): Official notification from the grantor indicating that the grant application has been approved and funding is forthcoming.

13. Outcome Measurements: Metrics used to assess the results or impact of a project, such as the number of people served or the degree of improvement in a particular area.

14. Proposal: A formal request for funding, outlining the project plan, budget, and the anticipated impact.

15. RFP (Request for Proposal): A document issued by a grantor inviting organizations to submit proposals for a specific project or program.

16. Seed Money: Initial funding used to start a new project or organization, often with the expectation that the project will become self-sustaining.

17. Sustainability Plan: A plan outlining how the project will continue and be funded after the grant period ends.

This glossary covers key terms that are frequently encountered in the grant application and management process. Familiarity with these terms will help grant seekers understand grant-related documents and communicate more effectively with grantors and stakeholders.

List of Resources and Tools

This section provides a curated list of resources and tools that can be invaluable for businesses seeking grant funding. These resources offer guidance, information, and practical support for the entire grant process, from finding opportunities to managing awarded funds.

1. Grant Databases and Search Platforms

- **Grants.gov**: The central repository for information on over 1,000 grant programs offered by all federal grant-making agencies in the United States.

- **Foundation Directory Online**: A comprehensive database providing access to an extensive list of philanthropic foundations.

- **GuideStar**: Offers information on non-profit organizations and is a useful tool for researching potential funders.

2. Proposal Writing Guides and Templates

- **The Foundation Center's Proposal Writing Short Course**: A free online course that provides a step-by-step guide to writing grant proposals.

- **GrantSpace by Candid**: Offers a variety of training, tools, and resources for writing effective grant proposals.

3. Budgeting and Financial Management Tools

- **QuickBooks Non-Profit**: Accounting software tailored for the financial management needs of non-profits and grant-funded organizations.

- **Excel or Google Sheets**: Useful for creating and managing budgets with customizable templates available.

4. Project Management Software

- **Trello**: A collaboration tool that organizes projects into boards, lists, and cards, ideal for managing grant projects.

- **Asana**: Project management software that helps teams coordinate and manage their work, from daily tasks to strategic initiatives.

5. Impact Measurement and Reporting Tools

- **SurveyMonkey**: An online survey tool useful for collecting data and feedback to measure the impact of projects.

- **Tableau**: A data visualization tool that can help in creating impactful reports and insights from project data.

6. Professional Associations and Networking Groups

- **Council on Foundations**: A non-profit leadership association of grant-making foundations and corporations, providing various resources and networking opportunities.

- **Grant Professionals Association**: Offers professional development and networking opportunities for individuals in the grants industry.

7. Legal and Compliance Information

- **Internal Revenue Service (IRS) - Charities and Non-Profits**: Provides information on federal tax laws and regulations for non-profits and charities in the U.S.

- **National Council of Nonprofits**: Offers resources and advocacy for non-profits, including compliance and ethical guidelines.

8. Online Learning Platforms

- **Coursera and Udemy**: Offer various online courses on grant writing, project management, and non-profit management.

9. Social Media Groups and Forums

- **LinkedIn Groups**: Such as "Non-Profit and Philanthropy" or "Grant Writers", for networking, advice, and sharing experiences.

- **Reddit Communities**: Subreddits like r/nonprofit provide a platform for discussion and advice on grant funding and non-profit management.

This list of resources and tools is designed to support businesses and organizations at every stage of the grant process. From identifying funding opportunities to managing and reporting on grant projects, these resources can help maximize the success and impact of your grant-funded endeavors.

Grant Funding Resources by Continent

North America

1. **National Endowment for the Arts (NEA)**

   - Website: arts.gov

2. **National Science Foundation (NSF)**

   - Website: nsf.gov

3. **Small Business Innovation Research (SBIR)**

   - Website: sbir.gov

4. **The Ford Foundation**

   - Website: fordfoundation.org

5. **The Rockefeller Foundation**

   - Website: rockefellerfoundation.org

6. **Bill & Melinda Gates Foundation**

   - Website: gatesfoundation.org

7. **The Canada Council for the Arts**

   - Website: canadacouncil.ca

8. **Canadian Institutes of Health Research (CIHR)**

   - Website: cihr-irsc.gc.ca

9. **Social Sciences and Humanities Research Council (SSHRC) - Canada**

   - Website: sshrc-crsh.gc.ca

10. **Natural Sciences and Engineering Research Council of Canada (NSERC)**

    - Website: nserc-crsng.gc.ca

11. **The Andrew W. Mellon Foundation**

   - Website: mellon.org

12. **The MacArthur Foundation**

   - Website: macfound.org

13. **Environmental Protection Agency (EPA) Grants - USA**

   - Website: epa.gov/grants

14. **The Robert Wood Johnson Foundation**

   - Website: rwjf.org

15. **The W.K. Kellogg Foundation**

   - Website: wkkf.org

16. **The Spencer Foundation (Education Research)**

   - Website: spencer.org

17. **The Walton Family Foundation**

   - Website: waltonfamilyfoundation.org

18. **The Michael & Susan Dell Foundation**

   - Website: msdf.org

19. **The Kresge Foundation**

   - Website: kresge.org

20. **The Annie E. Casey Foundation**

   - Website: aecf.org

21. **The Carnegie Corporation of New York**

   - Website: carnegie.org

22. **The John D. and Catherine T. MacArthur Foundation**

   - Website: macfound.org

23. **The William and Flora Hewlett Foundation**

- Website: hewlett.org

24. **The David and Lucile Packard Foundation**

- Website: packard.org

25. **The Open Society Foundations**

- Website: opensocietyfoundations.org

26. **The W.M. Keck Foundation**

- Website: wmkeck.org

27. **The Gordon and Betty Moore Foundation**

- Website: moore.org

28. **The Simons Foundation**

- Website: simonsfoundation.org

29. **The Broad Foundation**

- Website: broadfoundation.org

30. **The Doris Duke Charitable Foundation**

- Website: ddcf.org

31. **Knight Foundation**

- Website: kf.org

32. **The Conrad N. Hilton Foundation**

- Website: hiltonfoundation.org

33. **The Commonwealth Fund**

- Website: commonwealthfund.org

34. **The Pew Charitable Trusts**

- Website: pewtrusts.org

35. **The James Irvine Foundation**

- Website: irvine.org

36. **The Casey Family Programs**

- Website: casey.org

37. **The Bush Foundation**

- Website: bushfoundation.org

38. **The Daniels Fund**

- Website: danielsfund.org

39. **The Surdna Foundation**

- Website: surdna.org

40. **The Joyce Foundation**

- Website: joycefdn.org

41. **Lumina Foundation**

- Website: luminafoundation.org

42. **The Henry Luce Foundation**

- Website: hluce.org

43. **The Russell Sage Foundation**

- Website: russellsage.org

44. **The Richard King Mellon Foundation**

- Website: rkmf.org

45. **The McKnight Foundation**

- Website: mcknight.org

46. **The Hearst Foundations**

- Website: hearstfdn.org

47. **The Ewing Marion Kauffman Foundation**

- Website: kauffman.org

48. **The Robert Sterling Clark Foundation**

- Website: rsclark.org

49. **The Blavatnik Family Foundation**

    - Website: blavatnikfoundation.org

50. **The Children's Investment Fund Foundation (CIFF)**

    - Website: ciff.org

Europe

1. **European Commission Grants**

   - Website: ec.europa.eu

2. **The Wellcome Trust (UK)**

   - Website: wellcome.org

3. **The Volkswagen Foundation (Germany)**

   - Website: volkswagenstiftung.de

4. **The British Council**

   - Website: britishcouncil.org

5. **Nordic Council of Ministers (Nordic countries)**

   - Website: norden.org

6. **The Esmée Fairbairn Foundation (UK)**

   - Website: esmeefairbairn.org.uk

7. **The Leverhulme Trust (UK)**

   - Website: leverhulme.ac.uk

8. **Swiss National Science Foundation (Switzerland)**

   - Website: snf.ch

9. **Research Council of Norway (Norway)**

   - Website: forskningsradet.no

10. **Agence Nationale de la Recherche (ANR) (France)**

    - Website: anr.fr

11. **Deutsche Forschungsgemeinschaft (DFG) (Germany)**

    - Website: dfg.de

12. **Arts Council England (UK)**

    - Website: artscouncil.org.uk

13. **La Caixa Foundation (Spain)**

    - Website: fundacionlacaixa.org

14. **Innovate UK**

    - Website: gov.uk/government/organisations/innovate-uk

15. **Stiftung Mercator (Germany)**

    - Website: stiftung-mercator.de

16. **Horizon Europe**

    - Website: ec.europa.eu

17. **European Research Council (ERC)**

    - Website: erc.europa.eu

18. **The Nordic Culture Fund**

    - Website: nordiskkulturfond.org

19. **Kone Foundation (Finland)**

    - Website: koneensaatio.fi

20. **The Calouste Gulbenkian Foundation (Portugal)**

    - Website: gulbenkian.pt

21. **Riksbankens Jubileumsfond (Sweden)**

- Website: rj.se

22. **Fondazione Cariplo (Italy)**

- Website: fondazionecariplo.it

23. **The Sigrid Rausing Trust (UK)**

- Website: sigrid-rausing-trust.org

24. **The European Cultural Foundation**

- Website: culturalfoundation.eu

25. **The Goethe-Institut**

- Website: goethe.de

26. **The Velux Foundations (Denmark)**

- Website: veluxfoundations.dk

27. **The Dutch Research Council (NWO) (Netherlands)**

- Website: nwo.nl

28. **The Austrian Science Fund (FWF)**

- Website: fwf.ac.at

29. **The Wallenberg Foundations (Sweden)**

- Website: wallenberg.com

30. **The Finnish Cultural Foundation**

- Website: skr.fi

Africa

1. **The African Development Bank (AfDB)**

- Website: afdb.org

2. **The African Women's Development Fund (AWDF)**

    - Website: awdf.org

3. **The African Academy of Sciences (AAS)**

    - Website: aasciences.africa

4. **The United Nations Development Programme (UNDP) - Africa**

    - Website: africa.undp.org

5. **TrustAfrica**

    - Website: trustafrica.org

6. **The African Union Commission**

    - Website: au.int

7. **The Alliance for a Green Revolution in Africa (AGRA)**

    - Website: agra.org

8. **The MasterCard Foundation**

    - Website: mastercardfdn.org

9. **African Climate Foundation**

    - Website: africanclimatefoundation.org

10. **The Mandela Rhodes Foundation**

    - Website: mandelarhodes.org

11. **The Mo Ibrahim Foundation**

    - Website: moibrahimfoundation.org

12. **The Africa Grantmakers' Affinity Group (AGAG)**

    - Website: africagrantmakers.org

13. **The King Baudouin Foundation Africa**

    - Website: kbf-africa.org

14. **African Women in Agricultural Research and Development (AWARD)**

    - Website: awardfellowships.org

15. **The African Leadership Institute (AFLI)**

    - Website: alinstitute.org

16. **The African Research Universities Alliance (ARUA)**

    - Website: arua.org.za

17. **The African Capacity Building Foundation (ACBF)**

    - Website: acbf-pact.org

18. **The African Peacebuilding Network (APN)**

    - Website: ssrc.org/programs/apn

19. **The African Wildlife Foundation**

    - Website: awf.org

20. **The African Innovation Foundation**

    - Website: africaninnovation.org

21. **The United Nations Economic Commission for Africa (UNECA)**

    - Website: uneca.org

22. **The New Partnership for Africa's Development (NEPAD)**

    - Website: nepad.org

23. **African Economic Research Consortium (AERC)**

    - Website: aercafrica.org

24. **Ashoka Africa**

    - Website: africa.ashoka.org

25. **The African Union Research Grants**

- Website: au.int/en/aurg

26. **African Regional Intellectual Property Organization (ARIPO)**
    - Website: aripo.org

27. **The Energy and Environment Partnership Trust Fund (EEP Africa)**
    - Website: eepafrica.org

28. **The Global Fund for Children - Africa**
    - Website: globalfundforchildren.org

29. **The Aga Khan Foundation**
    - Website: akdn.org/our-agencies/aga-khan-foundation

30. **The West African Research Association (WARA)**
    - Website: bostonu.edu/wara

31. **The African Health Innovation Centre**
    - Website: ahic.org

32. **The African Leadership Academy**
    - Website: africanleadershipacademy.org

33. **Education Sub-Saharan Africa (ESSA)**
    - Website: essa-africa.org

34. **Foundation for African Development**
    - Website: ifad.org

35. **The Graca Machel Trust**
    - Website: gracamacheltrust.org

36. **The Africa Enterprise Challenge Fund (AECF)**
    - Website: aecfafrica.org

37. **The African Field Epidemiology Network (AFENET)**

- Website: afenet.net

38. **The African Population and Health Research Center (APHRC)**

    - Website: aphrc.org

39. **Investisseurs & Partenaires (I&P)**

    - Website: ietp.com

40. **TradeMark East Africa**

    - Website: trademarkea.com

41. **African Agricultural Technology Foundation (AATF)**

    - Website: aatf-africa.org

42. **The African Academy of Languages (ACALAN)**

    - Website: acalan.org

43. **Strategic Partnership for Higher Education Innovation and Reform (SPHEIR)**

    - Website: spheir.org.uk

44. **The African Union's Scientific, Technical and Research Commission**

    - Website: au.int/en/strc

45. **Pan African University (PAU)**

    - Website: pau-au.africa

46. **CODESRIA (Council for the Development of Social Science Research in Africa)**

    - Website: codesria.org

47. **Pan African Climate Justice Alliance**

    - Website: pacja.org

48. **African Union Scientific, Technical, and Research Commission**

- Website: au.int/en/strc

49. **The African Women's Development Fund**

   - Website: awdf.org

50. **The African Leadership Centre**

   - Website: africanleadershipcentre.org

51. **The East African Science and Technology Commission**

   - Website: easteco.org

52. **The African Legal Support Facility**

   - Website: aflsf.org

53. **The African Seed Access Index**

   - Website: tasai.org

54. **The African Economic Research Consortium**

   - Website: aercafrica.org

55. **The Next Einstein Forum**

   - Website: nef.org

56. **The Africa-EU Renewable Energy Cooperation Programme (RECP)**

   - Website: africa-eu-renewables.org

57. **The Forum for Agricultural Research in Africa (FARA)**

   - Website: faraafrica.org

58. **African Research and Resource Forum (ARRF)**

   - Website: arrforum.org

59. **The West African Research Association (WARA)**

   - Website: bostonu.edu/wara

60. **The Southern African Research and Documentation Centre (SARDC)**

- Website: sardc.net

Asia

1. **The Asia Foundation**

   - Website: asiafoundation.org

2. **The Asian Development Bank (ADB)**

   - Website: adb.org

3. **United Nations Development Programme (UNDP) - Asia-Pacific**

   - Website: asiapacific.undp.org

4. **The Japan Foundation**

   - Website: jpf.go.jp

5. **The Toyota Foundation**

   - Website: toyotafoundation.jp

6. **The Asia-Pacific Network for Global Change Research**

   - Website: apn-gcr.org

7. **The Bill & Melinda Gates Foundation - South Asia**

   - Website: gatesfoundation.org

8. **The Korea Foundation**

   - Website: kf.or.kr

9. **The Sasakawa Peace Foundation**

   - Website: spf.org

10. **The International Development Research Centre (IDRC) - Asia**

    - Website: idrc.ca

11. **The Asia-Europe Foundation (ASEF)**

    - Website: asef.org

12. **The King Abdullah International Foundation**

    - Website: kaust.edu.sa

13. **The Asian Cultural Council**

    - Website: asianculturalcouncil.org

14. **The Lee Foundation**

    - Website: leefoundation.sg

15. **The Asia Research Center**

    - Website: asia-research-center.com

16. **Ratan Tata Trust (India)**

    - Website: tatatrusts.org

17. **The Hong Kong Jockey Club Charities Trust (Hong Kong)**

    - Website: charities.hkjc.com

18. **The Asia-Pacific Foundation of Canada**

    - Website: asiapacific.ca

19. **The Nippon Foundation (Japan)**

    - Website: nippon-foundation.or.jp

20. **The Ramon Magsaysay Award Foundation (Philippines)**

    - Website: rmaward.asia

21. **The Habibie Center (Indonesia)**

    - Website: habibiecenter.or.id

22. **O.P. Jindal Global University Research Grants (India)**

- Website: jgu.edu.in

23. **The Asia Foundation - Korea**

- Website: asiafoundation.or.kr

24. **The Asia-Pacific Network for Sustainable Forest Management and Rehabilitation (APFNet)**

- Website: apfnet.cn

25. **The Mitsubishi Corporation Fund for Europe and Africa**

- Website: mcfund-ea.org

26. **The Murata Science Foundation (Japan)**

- Website: murata.com

27. **The Toyota Environmental Activities Grant Program (Japan)**

- Website: toyota.com

28. **The Sumitomo Foundation (Japan)**

- Website: sumitomo.or.jp

29. **The Liu Bie Ju Foundation (China)**

- Website: lbjfoundation.com

30. **The Chiang Ching-kuo Foundation for International Scholarly Exchange (Taiwan)**

- Website: cckf.org

31. **The King Baudouin Foundation (KBF) - Asia**

- Website: kbs-frb.be

32. **The Li Ka Shing Foundation (Hong Kong)**

- Website: lksf.org

33. **The TATA Trusts (India)**

- Website: tatatrusts.org

34. **The Reliance Foundation (India)**

- Website: reliancefoundation.org

35. **The Aga Khan Development Network**

- Website: akdn.org

36. **DBS Foundation (Singapore)**

- Website: dbs.com/dbsfoundation

37. **The Maybank Foundation (Malaysia)**

- Website: maybankfoundation.com

38. **The Hyundai Motor Chung Mong-Koo Foundation (South Korea)**

- Website: foundation.hyundai.com

39. **The LG Yonam Foundation (South Korea)**

- Website: lgyonam.org

40. **The Lotte Foundation (South Korea)**

- Website: lottefoundation.or.kr

41. **The Posco TJ Park Foundation (South Korea)**

- Website: postf.org

42. **The Shinnyo-en Foundation (Japan)**

- Website: shinnyoenfoundation.org

43. **The Toyota Foundation (Japan)**

- Website: toyotafound.or.jp

44. **The Seiji Togo Memorial Sompo Japan Nipponkoa Museum of Art (Japan)**

- Website: sompo-museum.org

45. **The Canon Foundation (Japan)**

- Website: canonfoundation.org

South America

1. **The Inter-American Development Bank (IDB)**

   - Website: iadb.org

2. **The Latin American Council of Social Sciences (CLACSO)**

   - Website: clacso.org

3. **The Latin American Development Bank (CAF)**

   - Website: caf.com

4. **The Amazon Environmental Research Institute (IPAM) - Brazil**

   - Website: ipam.org.br

5. **The Andean Development Corporation (CAF)**

   - Website: caf.com

6. **The Lemann Foundation (Brazil)**

   - Website: lemannfoundation.org

7. **The Avina Foundation**

   - Website: avina.net

8. **The International Institute for Sustainable Development (IISD) - Latin America**

   - Website: iisd.org

9. **The OAS Partnerships Program for Education and Training (PAEC)**

   - Website: oas.org/en/paec

10. **The Ford Foundation - Brazil Office**

    - Website: fordfoundation.org

11. **The IDRC Regional Office for Latin America and the Caribbean**

   - Website: idrc.ca

12. **The Fundación para la Conservación del Bosque Chaqueño (Argentina)**

   - Website: bosquechaqueno.org.ar

13. **The Fundación para la Investigación y Desarrollo Ambiental (FIDA) - Ecuador**

   - Website: fundacionfida.org

14. **The Fundação de Amparo à Pesquisa do Estado de São Paulo (FAPESP) - Brazil**

   - Website: fapesp.br

15. **The Fundación para la Promoción de la Investigación y la Tecnología (FINTEC) - Paraguay**

   - Website: fintec.org.py

Oceania

1. **The Pacific Islands Forum Secretariat (PIFS)**

   - Website: forumsec.org

2. **The Australian Government Grants Directory**

   - Website: grants.gov.au

3. **The New Zealand Ministry of Business, Innovation, and Employment (MBIE)**

   - Website: mbie.govt.nz

4. **The Australian Research Council (ARC)**

   - Website: arc.gov.au

5. **The Pacific Development and Conservation Trust (PDCT) - New Zealand**

   - Website: dunedin.govt.nz

6. **The Australian Ethical Foundation**

   - Website: australianethical.com.au

7. **The Indigenous Land and Sea Corporation (ILSC) - Australia**

   - Website: ilc.gov.au

8. **The Department of Foreign Affairs and Trade (DFAT) - Australia**

   - Website: dfat.gov.au

9. **The Foundation for Rural and Regional Renewal (FRRR) - Australia**

   - Website: frrr.org.au

10. **The Pacific Community (SPC)**

    - Website: spc.int

Antarctica

1. **Efficiency for Access Research and Development Fund**: This fund invites organizations to apply for research and development funding to support sustainability efforts in November 2023.

2. **Erase Indifference Challenge 2024**: This initiative aims to find and fund innovative projects that combat indifference and promote concrete actions, starting at the Auschwitz Pledge Foundation.

3. **Youth Hub Seed Grant Programme**: The International AIDS Society invites proposals for innovation projects addressing the needs of young people affected by HIV from March to August 2024.

4. **International Young Eco-Hero Awards**: Action For Nature is seeking nominations to recognize young individuals aged 8 to 16 for their successful environmental initiatives.

5. **DRL Lifeline: Embattled CSOs Assistance Fund**: The U.S. Department of State offers funding for projects that support civil society and counter closing civic space.

Templates and Sample Documents

These documents are essential tools for preparing grant applications. They include:

1. Grant Proposal Template: A structured outline to guide you in creating a well-organized grant proposal.

2. Budget Template: A financial planning template to help you create a comprehensive budget for your project.

3. Sample Grant Proposals: Real-life grant proposals that have been successful, allowing you to see what works.

4. Letters of Inquiry Template: Templates for introductory letters to potential funders (Check Candid's resources).

5. Impact Reports Samples: Samples of reports that demonstrate the impact of funded projects, useful for reporting requirements.

6. Project Plans Template: Templates for outlining your project's goals, objectives, and timeline.

7. Evaluation Plans Samples: Samples for assessing the success of your project.

These online resources will serve as practical guides and examples to streamline your grant application process and increase your chances of securing funding.

Conclusion

In conclusion, this comprehensive guide has provided you with a wealth of knowledge and practical insights into the world of grant funding for businesses. Let's recap the key points:

- Grant funding is a valuable financial resource for businesses of all sizes and sectors.

- Understanding the types of grants, eligibility criteria, and the application process is crucial.

- Crafting a compelling proposal, avoiding common mistakes, and effective fund management are vital steps.

- Building relationships with funders, leveraging grants for further funding, and partnerships are advanced strategies.

- Stay updated on emerging trends and the impact of technology on grant seeking for the future.

As you embark on your grant-seeking journey, remember that persistence and creativity are your allies. Never underestimate the positive impact your business can make with the support of grants.

References

1. Technical Writer HQ. "6 Best Grant Writing Books 2024." Technical Writer HQ. https://www.technicalwriterhq.com/best-grant-writing-books/ (Accessed January 12, 2024).

2. Grant Writing Academy. "The Top Trends and Changes in Grant Funding in 2023." Grant Writing Academy. https://www.grantwritingacad.org/trends-and-changes-in-grant-funding-2023/ (Accessed January 12, 2024).

3. Instrumentl. "35 Grant Statistics for 2023: The Ultimate List." Instrumentl. https://www.instrumentl.com/35-grant-statistics-for-2023 (Accessed January 12, 2024).

4. NonProfit PRO. "Emerging Grantmaking Trends: What You Need to Know." NonProfit PRO. https://www.nonprofitpro.com/article/emerging-grantmaking-trends/ (Accessed January 12, 2024).

5. Noveck, Beth, Andrew Young, and Andrew Miller. "Innovations in Open Grantmaking." Candid Learning for Funders. September 27, 2016. https://learningforfunders.candid.org/innovations-in-open-grantmaking (Accessed January 12, 2024).

6. Foundation Source. "Articles and Resources on Philanthropy and Grantmaking." Foundation Source. https://www.foundationsource.com/blog/ (Accessed January 12, 2024).